SOCK CLUB

Join the Knitting Adventure

Charlene Schurch
and Beth Parrott

Martingale®
& COMPANY

DEDICATION

To sock knitters, and all who contributed, past and present, to the strength, variety and creativity of the extended sock-knitting community. They include technical innovators, spinners, dyers, sock-club sponsors, pattern designers, enthusiastic sock knitters, grateful sock wearers, and most especially, our sock-knitting ancestors, who turned the first heel, Kitchenered the first toe and started us on a happy journey with warm feet.

Sock Club: Join the Knitting Adventure
© 2010 by Charlene Schurch and Beth Parrott

Martingale®
& C O M P A N Y

Martingale & Company®
20205 144th Ave. NE
Woodinville, WA 98072-8478 USA
www.martingale-pub.com

Printed in China
15 14 13 12 11 10   8 7 6 5 4 3 2 1

Library of Congress
Cataloging-in-Publication Data
is available upon request.

ISBN: 978-1-56477-936-6

Mission Statement
Dedicated to providing quality products and service to inspire creativity.

Credits

President & CEO ♥ Tom Wierzbicki

Editor in Chief ♥ Mary V. Green

Managing Editor ♥ Tina Cook

Developmental Editor ♥ Karen Costello Soltys

Technical Editor ♥ Ursula Reikes

Copy Editor ♥ Marcy Heffernan

Design Director ♥ Stan Green

Production Manager ♥ Regina Girard

Illustrator ♥ Laurel Strand

Cover & Text Designer ♥ Regina Girard

Photographer ♥ Brent Kane

CONTENTS

page 33

page 54

page 19

INTRODUCTION

In the 1950s, when I was a young girl, I remember Mother belonged to a sewing circle. Once a month she would gather in the evening with other women who did various kinds of needlework. They would share dessert, conversation, and their creativity and have an evening without children and chores. I remember loving the idea of it, and since I, too, did needlework, I wondered when I would be able to join in. Since high school, I've belonged to a variety of women's groups and fiber guilds. I always look forward to the opportunity to get to know others with similar interests, share ideas, and give and receive assistance and support. My favorite way to spend a Saturday afternoon is with other knitters at my local yarn shop.

Thanks to the Internet, the twenty-first century has brought new versions of the sewing circle. They include folks worldwide coming together in groups—ranging from a few individuals to many thousands—without leaving the comfort of their homes. For socks, these circles include the Yahoo Socknitters, with over 10,000 members who share information, ideas, and advice. Both as a part of Socknitters and separately, groups of knitters decided to knit the same pattern and created Knit-Alongs (KAL) to be able to simultaneously share their experiences in even more detail.

About the same time, 2001, yarn shops (Internet and local) and independent dyers saw an opportunity to package sock kits, including yarn, pattern, and accessories, which were sent to the participating knitter on a regular basis, monthly or bimonthly, and the "sock club" was born. Often the yarn and/or pattern were available to members only—at least for a limited period of time. Sock knitters were delighted to receive each surprise package, motivated to try new skills, and encouraged to work with new and unique materials, all the while with the support of the sponsor and often with a member KAL group to rely on as well.

In spring 2008, Charlene and I noted the creativity and originality of so many socks we saw shared in sock clubs, at yarn shops, on the Internet, and in KALs, including those emerging on Ravelry (an online community of knitters, crocheters, designers, spinners, dyers, and some weavers that provides a place to keep track of yarn, tools, and pattern information as well as a chance to turn to others for inspiration and support). The variety of designs and techniques used, as well as the range of skill levels, were impressive. When we realized how popular sock clubs were, we thought a book featuring socks from some of the clubs would be a good idea. We sent out a call for submissions and received a large number of excellent designs. The hardest part was choosing which to include in our book.

One of the special blessings of our process was the significant number of designs that came from sock clubs sponsored by independent dyers (see "Dyers" on page 79). Their yarns are striking and unique—most of the samples pictured are one-of-a-kind yarns. You may be able to order yarn that is similar, though it's likely that no two hanks will be exactly the same. Variation is to be expected and variety is the spice!

All of the socks in this book were originally designed for sock clubs or KALs. Many of the designers are highly skilled professionals; for a few, this will be their first published design. They are from all corners of the United States (Connecticut, California, Oregon, and Florida) and the Island of Guernsey in the English Channel. We are delighted by the variety and impressed by the creativity of each one. We hope that you will enjoy knitting them as much as we enjoyed gathering them together.

—Beth Parrott
Charleston, South Carolina

Knitting has largely been a solitary occupation for me—with lots of knitting on the couch for a book deadline or working on a personal project while watching television. The exceptions have been some guild sit-and-knit occasions as well as knitting with my mother. It's always interesting to see what everyone else is knitting when knitting in a group, because the diversity is exciting.

With the advent of the Internet and Ravelry we now have the ability to be knitting the same project as many others and to see how similar and how different the results can be when we all knit from the same pattern. Even though we know that there are more active knitters now than a few years ago, it can still feel like we're knitting alone. Joining a Sock Club is a wonderful way to feel part of a larger knitting community, as well as enjoy the marvelous surprise of receiving lovely yarn and a new sock pattern several times a year. We hope you will enjoy this wonderful collection of sock patterns and new yarn sources for your knitting pleasure.

—Charlene Schurch
Middletown, Connecticutt

MAKING IT YOUR SIZE

As a sock knitter, you sometimes see a picture of a sock and it's love at first sight. Then you check out the pattern—and it's "one size fits most" (but not *you*). There are many alternatives to make almost any sock your size. We hope you will follow along and review the options for converting the pattern you love to the size you need. We have done this most of our lives. Charlene wears a size 5½ narrow shoe and long ago tired of having floppy socks. Beth has worn a 10½ EE since age 13 or so. As a teenager, she learned to knit socks to avoid wearing men's athletic socks to school.

A number of socks submitted for this book were originally available to sock club or Knit-Along (KAL) members as a single-sized pattern. In most cases, the designer was able to add two, three, or even more sizes to the patterns for this book. Where that is the case, we sincerely hope that the size you require is one of the sizes in the pattern. However, if you encounter a pattern in a sock club or book where a women's medium is the only size given, we hope this section will prepare you with the tools and skills needed to adapt the pattern yourself. The patterns in this book include examples of many ways to design additional sizes. Sizing methods are listed here in order of most to least commonly used.

Ⓖ Changing the **gauge** by changing the needle size or the yarn weight (Serendipity, Ariel, Cozy Cables, Acorn Stash, and Teatime)

Ⓝ Changing the **number** of pattern repeats (Indiana Jones, Beaded Lattice, Ariel, Havana Lace, Daydreamer, Gluttony, Rainbow Swirl, Wavy, Rainbow over Lahaina, Reims, and Rocks and Trails)

Ⓢ Changing the **spacing** (number of stitches) between pattern elements (Roof Ridge, I Love Gansey, Blush, and Zigs and Zags)

Ⓑ Changing the number of **background** stitches around a centered motif (Reina, Gothic Temptress, and Celtic Spirit)

Ⓔ Changing **elements** within a repeat (Serendipity, Roof Ridge, and Low Country Light)

Ⓜ Adding a small **motif** between pattern repeats (Teatime)

Some of the socks in this book have pattern repeats of two to eight stitches. Others have large pattern repeats of 12, 16, or more stitches and are much more difficult to design in multiple sizes, at least in sizes that are useful to real people. Our goal is to help you learn strategies and techniques from the way these designers modified their patterns, so that you may apply these same strategies and techniques to other patterns. Stay with us, and we'll run through a gamut of alternatives. Strategies will vary, depending on the situation; remember to keep an open mind about all of the options.

Changing the Gauge by Changing the Needle Size Ⓖ

If the pattern you admire is somewhat close to your size, but not quite right, the simplest change to make is to adjust the gauge. One way to do that is to change the size of the needle. Let's say the pattern is for a standard size 8 shoe (women's medium), with 64 stitches, knit on size 2 needles at about 7½ stitches per inch. That's a sock circumference of 8½" for a shoe size 8 or 8½. But you wear a size 6½ or 7 shoe!

First, let me say the nasty word—you have to *swatch*. If you do, it's likely that going down to a size 1 needle will give you 8 stitches per inch; those 64 stitches will equal about 8" circumference, which is just about what you need. If size 1 needles don't get you there, you may have to try size 0, but at least you're able to find a way to knit the pattern.

Similarly, if you wear size 10 shoes, you should be in the right ballpark with the same sock knit on size 3 needles at about 7 stitches per inch. Keep in mind that socks that are knit more loosely may not wear as well as those knit densely. So when increasing needle size, combine that change with a change in yarn (see below).

In this book most patterns use a fingering-weight yarn (**1**)—yet the yardage of a 100-gram skein varies from 480 yards to 310 yards. Remembering that the lesser-yardage yarn will be somewhat thicker; we should choose a yarn with fewer yards to produce a dense wearable fabric. We can also take this option in the other direction. By combining a thinner fingering-weight yarn with the smaller needles, we can avoid a sock fabric that is too dense or too hard to work on.

Changing the Gauge by Changing the Yarn Weight (G)

When a pattern is a Women's Medium (size 8 or 8½ shoe), it can be a pretty easy change to a Woman's Extra Large. Most patterns are written for fingering-weight yarn at about 7½ stitches per inch. The same pattern knit in sport-weight yarn on size 3 needles gives a gauge of 6½ stitches per inch, which is almost exactly the 10" sock circumference needed.

Let's review the math. The original pattern had 64 stitches at a gauge of 7½ stitches per inch; 64 stitches divided by stitches per inch equals an 8½" foot circumference. With a wee bit of ease, this sock will fit shoe size 8 (8⅜" foot circumference) or shoe size 8½ (8½" foot circumference).

If we knit the same 64 stitches at sport-weight gauge of 6½ stitches per inch, the 64 stitches divided by 6½ sts per inch equals 9⅞", which with a wee bit of ease brings us right up to the required 10" foot circumference.

First, look at the typical knit gauges for each weight of yarn and calculate the conversion. Remember that for good wear, socks are typically knit on smaller needles than those indicated on the ball band. Second, swatch

the yarn you intend to use with several different needle sizes. Check your swatches to see which one achieved the gauge you require and a fabric dense enough to wear well. Finally, knit with the new yarn and needles and enjoy the pattern you converted.

There are two patterns in this book that suggest changing needle size and/or yarn weight as additional alternatives to fine-tune sock sizes; see "Options for Larger Sizes" in Serendipity on page 9 and "Note on Sizing" in Ariel on page 40. Two socks, Cozy Cables on page 60 and Acorn Stash on page 63, have leg patterns with such wide repeats and complex patterning that changing the leg pattern to a different size was out of the question. In both cases, you must change the size by changing the gauge. Changing the needle size will achieve modest changes in the sock size, but more significant changes will require changing the yarn weight and the needle size in combination.

Changing the Number of Pattern Repeats (N)

The next option for changing sock size is to resize the pattern. If the pattern has a moderate repeat of six or eight stitches or fewer, this is likely the best way to go. Changing the size most frequently means adding or subtracting two pattern repeats so you do not have to split the stitches of a single repeat between the instep and the heel. If it's not possible to add or subtract two repeats, you can make up for the half repeat with several stockinette stitches at each side of the instep.

The largest group of patterns in this book add or subtract repeats to make the design available in multiple sizes. They are grouped together (beginning on page 33) and can be used as a model for how this is done. Reims on page 56 is an example where only one repeat is added and stockinette stitch is used to balance the instep.

Working out the math for a smaller or larger sock can be challenging, but you really don't need to do it if you use a sock calculator. Several are available online. Our favorite is Mary Moran's *Sockcalc.* available as a download from her website for your personal use at:

http://www.needletrax.com/mysocks.htm

Others that we're aware of are:

www.panix.com/~ilaine/socks.html

www.princeton.edu/~ezb/sockform.html

If you're likely to modify sock sizes frequently and want a variety of options including knitting from the cuff down, knitting from the toe up, choosing your own heels, etc., consider an investment in sock-knitting software.

Mary Moran's is called "The Sole Solution," and Carole Wulster's is called "Sock Wizard." They are available from their respective websites and are also sold at many yarn shops.

For an extensive collection of socks designed using the technique of changing the number of pattern repeats, see *Sensational Knitted Socks* (Martingale & Company, 2005) and *More Sensational Knitted Socks* (Martingale & Company, 2007) by Charlene Schurch.

Changing the Spacing (Number of Stitches) between Pattern Elements

Often a sock design has one or more prominent elements, such as cables, around the leg of the sock. These elements are usually separated by two or more knit stitches or purl stitches. Increasing or decreasing the number of background stitches will change the leg circumference. Examples of socks that use this option are I Love Gansey on page 16 and Blush on page 19.

A slightly different variation of this option is shown in Roof Ridge on page 10. In this example, one section of the very long pattern repeat adds additional knit stitches. Serendipity on page 8 also adds knit stitches, but at the edge of the repeat.

Changing the Number of Background Stitches around a Centered Motif B

There are three examples in the book of socks that have a single large motif. They are Celtic Spirit on page 30, Reina on page 25, and Gothic Temptress on page 28. In each sock, the cable or double cable motif is centered on the front or back of the sock, and the remainder of the sock is worked in stockinette stitch or ribbing. Within limits, increasing or decreasing the amount of stockinette stitch or ribbing to the required number of stitches for the size desired should be relatively simple. Two important considerations should apply. First, the gauge of the motif is likely different from the gauge of the stockinette stitch or ribbing. Starting with the stated sock circumference, add or subtract stitches based on the gauge of stockinette stitch or ribbing to achieve the desired measurement. Second, the sock size must not be decreased to the point that the motif becomes more than half of the total stitches. This would create a problem when dividing the stitches for the heel and instep.

Changing Elements within a Repeat E

When Beth was designing Low Country Light on page 12, she chose a pattern with a 16-stitch repeat. At 7¾ stitches per inch, it works out about right for a Women's Medium sock. BUT, she was baffled about how to get other sizes. The pattern didn't lend itself to being split up on the instep. Adding or subtracting two repeats (4") yielded sizes that would only work for a leprechaun or Shreck. She nearly gave up and thought it had to be a single-size pattern.

Then, while she was working on ideas for this section of the book, she had an AHA! moment. One section of the pattern repeat consists of three adjacent three-stitch mini-cables. If one was removed and only two cables were used, the pattern repeat dropped to 13 stitches. With four repeats and a total of 52 stitches, we are just under 7", very close to the right size for a Child's Large or Women's Small sock. Adding a fourth cable brings the pattern repeat to 19 stitches. With four repeats and the same gauge, we're at 9½", just about right for a Women's Extra Large.

Adding a Small Motif between Pattern Repeats M

Teatime on page 66 is a lovely mosaic sock. The mosaic pattern is large, and each repeat is half of the sock. The designer cleverly adds a small lattice panel to each side of the sock to make it larger. The opportunities to apply this device to other situations seem almost unlimited.

We certainly hope you will enjoy the collection of patterns we have brought together here—a wonderful assortment of unique socks designed by new and experienced sock designers. We also hope the opportunity to learn ways that additional sizes can be designed will expand your knitting horizons in unexpected ways.

—*Charlene and Beth*

SERENDIPITY

Designed by Ellie Putz

♥ **SKILL LEVEL:** Intermediate ◼◼◼◻◻ ♥ **SIZE:** Women's Medium (see "Options for Larger Sizes" at right above) ♥ **FINISHED FOOT CIRCUMFERENCE:** Approx 8" ♥ **SIZING METHOD:** Ⓔ Ⓖ

This pattern developed while Ellie was trying to knit "Synesthesia Socks," which were designed by Sarah of Bella Knitting. She says that somehow she just couldn't pay attention to the pattern and started to improvise. This pattern, Serendipity, was the result.

Materials

1 skein of Creamy Sock from Crazy4Dyeing; Ellie Putz, dyer (80% milk protein, 20% wool; 100 g; 360 yds) in color Autumn Mist (**2**)

2 circular needles in size 1 (2.25 mm) or size required for gauge

Tapestry needle

Gauge

8½ sts = 1" in serendipity patt worked in the rnd

Serendipity Pattern

(Chart at right)

Written insructions below are for 68-st CO. For 76-st CO, see chart.

Rnd 1: *K1, K2tog, K5, YO, K1, YO K5, ssk, K1; rep from *.

Rnds 2, 4, 6, 8, and 10: Knit.

Rnd 3: *K1, K2tog, K4, YO, K3, YO, K4, ssk, K1; rep from *.

Rnd 5: *K1, K2tog, K3, YO, K5, YO, K3, ssk, K1; rep from *.

Rnd 7: *K1, K2tog, K2, YO, K7, YO, K2, ssk, K1; rep from *.

Rnd 9: *K1, K2tog, K1, YO, K9, YO, K1, ssk, K1; rep from *.

Rnd 11: *K1, K2tog, YO, K11, YO, ssk, K1; rep from *.

Rnd 12: Knit.

Rep rnds 1–12 for patt.

Cuff

CO 68 sts loosely. Divide sts evenly on 2 circular needles; 34 heel sts on needle 1, and 34 instep sts on needle 2. Join, being careful not to twist sts. Work P1, K1 tbl ribbing for 12 rows (approx ¾").

Leg

Knit 1 rnd. Beg Serendipity patt and work 5 complete vertical reps, then work rnds 1–11 once more (approx 6⅝").

Short-Row Heel

Heel is worked back and forth on the 34 sts on needle 1.

Row 1 (RS): Knit until 1 st rems, turn.

Row 2: YO, purl until 1 st rems, turn.

Row 3: YO, knit to first st/YO pair, turn.

Row 4: YO, purl to first st/YO pair, turn.

Rep rows 3 and 4 until each end of needle has one st on the end, and 11 st/YO pairs. This will occur when you are ready to beg a RS row.

Row 5 (RS): Knit to first st/YO pair. K1 (st from the st/YO pair), K2tog, turn.

Row 6: YO, purl to first st/YO pair. P1 (st from the st/YO pair), ssp, turn.

Row 7: YO, knit to first YO and K3tog (knit 2 YOs and following st tog), turn.

Row 8: YO, purl to first YO, sssp (purl 2 YOs and following st tog), turn.

Rep rows 7 and 8 until last st on each end is worked. This will be a WS row.

Foot

Transition Rows

Needle 1 (sole): YO, knit to last st (last YO) on this needle. Sl this st to needle 2, which is holding instep sts.

Needle 2 (instep): Knit the transferred st tog with the first instep st, counting it as first patt st of rnd 1. Work instep in patt to last st. Move YO at beg of heel needle to instep needle and ssk tog with last instep st, counting it as last patt st of rnd 1.

Cont needle 1 in St st and needle 2 in patt until 7½" or 2" less than desired foot length.

Toe

Rnd 1: Knit.

Rnd 2: K1, ssk, knit to last 3 sts, K2tog, K1. Rep for both needles.

Work rnds 1 and 2 until 10 total sts rem.

Graft toe sts tog using Kitchener st (see page 73) or desired grafting method. Weave in ends.

Serendipity Pattern

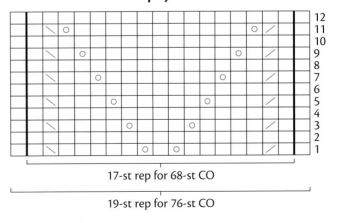

17-st rep for 68-st CO

19-st rep for 76-st CO

Key

☐	K	╲	ssk
╱	K2tog	⊙	YO

ROOF RIDGE

Designed by Emily B. Miller

♥ **SKILL LEVEL:** Intermediate ⬛⬛⬛◻ ♥ **SIZE:** Women's Medium (Women's Extra Large, Men's Extra Large)
♥ **FINISHED FOOT CIRCUMFERENCE:** Approx 8 (9½, 11)" ♥ **SIZING METHOD:** 🅔 🆂

When Emily first saw the Eclectic colorway from Chewy Spaghetti, she knew it would be great fun, but also a challenge to design a sock that could contain those bright colors harmoniously. Many stitch patterns would be lost in such a colorway. So the design concept was to create a sock that displayed all of the best aspects of brightly hand-painted yarn and none of the pitfalls, like pooling or obscured stitch patterns. Therefore, although the pattern was especially intended for the Eclectic colorway, it can be used for many of the gorgeous hand-painted yarns that are readily available.

Materials

1 skein of Handpainted Spaghetti
II from Chewy Spaghetti; Khris
Rogers, dyer (100% superwash
merino, 110 g; 320 yds/293 m) in
color Eclectic (**2**)

2 circular needles (24" long) in size 1½
(2.5 mm) or size required for gauge

4 stitch markers

Tapestry needle

Gauge

8 sts = 1" in St st worked in the rnd

Special Abbreviations

LLI (left-leaning increase): Use left
needle to lift left leg of st that is
2 sts below the st on right needle,
knit lifted leg through its back loop.

RLI (right-leaning increase): Use
right needle to lift right leg of st
below st on left needle, knit into
lifted leg.

Cuff

CO 60 (72, 84) sts. Divide sts evenly
on 2 circular needles; 30 (36, 42) sts
on each needle. Join, being careful
not to twist sts. Work K1, P1 ribbing
for 2". Needle 1 is first half of rnd
and will be back of leg and sole.
Needle 2 has rem sts that will be
front of leg and top of foot.

Leg

Set-up rnd: Needles 1 and 2: [K10 (12,
14), pm] twice, knit to end.

Rnd 1

Needles 1 and 2: Ssk, knit to marker,
RLI, sm, *P1, sl 1 wyif; rep from * to 2
sts before marker, P2, sm, LLI, knit to
2 sts before end of needle, K2tog.

Rnd 2: Knit.

Rnd 3

Needles 1 and 2: Ssk, knit to marker,
RLI, sm, P2, *sl 1 wyif, P1; rep from
* to marker, sm, LLI, knit to 2 sts
before end of needle, K2tog.

Rnd 4: Knit.

Rep rnds 1–4 until leg measures 7" or
desired length from CO edge. End
with rnd 3.

Afterthought Heel Setup

This sock has an afterthought heel
to avoid interrupting the bold
patterning of the yarn and to
easily allow the peak of the st patt
to cont onto the heel.

Using scrap yarn, knit across needle 1,
removing markers as you come to
them. Slide the needle through the
sts (or sl them back onto left needle
tip) and return to beg of rnd. With
main yarn, knit 1 rnd in St st. (The
scrap yarn will hold 1 row of live sts
to pick up later for the heel.)

Rnd 5

Needle 1: Knit.

Needle 2: Ssk, knit to marker, RLI, sm,
*P1, sl 1 wyif; rep from * to 2 sts
before marker, P2, sm, LLI, knit to 2
sts before end of needle, K2tog.

Rnd 6: Knit.

Rnd 7

Needle 1: Knit.

Needle 2: Ssk, knit to marker, RLI,
sm, P2, *sl 1 wyif, P1; rep from * to
marker, sm, LLI, knit to 2 sts before
end of needle, K2tog.

Rnd 8: Knit.

Rep rnds 5–8 until sock length after
row of scrap yarn is appropriate
for length of your foot between
base of heel cup (the point directly
below ankle bone) and the beg of
big toe. End with rnd 8. The sample
sock (Women's Medium) has a 5"
foot length between base of heel
cup and beg of toe.

Toe Shaping

Rnd 9

Needle 1: Ssk, knit to 2 sts before end
of needle, K2tog.

Needle 2: Ssk, knit to marker, RLI, sm,
P2tog, * P1, sl 1 wyif; rep from * until
2 sts before marker, P2tog, sm, LLI,
knit to 2 sts before end of needle,
K2tog.

Rnd 10: Knit.

Rep rnds 9 and 10 until only 4 sts rem
between markers. End with rnd 10.

Rnd 11

Needle 1: Ssk, knit to 2 sts before end
of needle, K2tog.

Needle 2: Ssk, knit to marker, RLI,
remove marker, P2tog twice,
remove marker, LLI, knit to 2 sts
before end of needle, K2tog.

Rnd 12: Knit.

Rnd 13

Needles 1 and 2: Ssk, knit to 2 sts
before end of needle, K2tog.

Rnd 14: Knit.

Rep rnds 13 and 14 until 20 sts rem on
each needle (40 sts total).

Rep rnd 13 only until 10 sts rem on
each needle (20 sts total).

Graft toe sts closed using Kitchener
st (see page 73) or desired grafting
method. Weave in ends.

Afterthought Heel

To pick up sts for heel, carefully
remove scrap yarn, transferring
each live st to its needle as you
go (place sts for leg on needle 1
and sts for foot on needle 2). You
will have 30 (36, 42) sts on needle 1
and only 29 (35, 41) sts on needle 2.
Attach yarn at beg of needle 1. As
you work first rnd, be sure sts are
properly mounted on needles so
they do not become twisted.

Work following rnd to even up
number of sts.

Needle 1: *K10 (12, 14), pm; rep from *
once, knit to end.

Needle 2: PU 1 st in gap between
needles, knit 29 (35, 41)—30 (36,
42) sts.

Work heel cup using instructions for
rnds 9–14 of toe shaping, EXCEPT
that instructions for needle 2 will
be used on needle 1 and vice versa
since st patt at back of heel is beg
of rnd and St st dec are on second
needle at bottom of foot. When
10 sts rem on each needle (20
sts total), graft toe sts tog using
Kitchener st (see page 73) or desired
grafting method. Weave in ends.

LOW COUNTRY LIGHT

Designed by Beth Parrott

♥ **SKILL LEVEL:** Expert ◼◼◼◻ ♥ **SIZE:** Child's Large/Women's Small (Women's Medium, Women's Extra Large) ♥ **FINISHED FOOT CIRCUMFERENCE:** Approx 6½" (8", 9½") ♥ **SIZING METHOD:** Ⓔ

The colors of Unique Sheep Gradiance yarns remind Beth of South Carolina's Low Country—the colors of the light are always changing as they interact with the landscape. The colors chosen for this sock remind her of late afternoon on a stormy day. In this stitch pattern, the twisted stitches represent how Low Country light shimmers, especially when reflected off the bays and inlets, and the lattice represents Charleston's renowned gates and grillwork.

Materials

1 regular (regular, big foot) set* of 4 Gradiance colors in Sushi Sock from Unique Sheep [60% superwash wool, 30% bamboo, 10% nylon; 100 (100, 150) g total; 388 (388, 582) yds total] in color Wild Parrott from the Gradiance collection

Set of 5 double-pointed needles in size 0 (2.00 mm) and size 1 (2.25 mm) or size required for gauge

Tapestry needle

A regular set contains 4 skeins, each 25 g; the big foot set contains 4 skeins, each 37.5 g.

ABOUT GRADIANCE YARNS

The Gradiance dyeing technique was invented by Kelly Eells, co-owner of The Unique Sheep, and is exclusive to the Unique Sheep. She developed a way of dyeing yarn so that as a set of four skeins is used, your project will gradually change from one hand-painted color to the next. Some sets have a dramatic shift in color, and others have more subtle transition. The gradually transitioned sets work well to show off more complicated stitch patterns and lacework because each skein is "almost" solid.

Gauge

8 sts = 1" in St st worked in the rnd on larger needles

Ribbing Pattern

Rnd 1

Small: *K2, P2, K1, P2, K1, P2, K2, P1; rep from * to end.

Medium: *K2, P1, K2, P2, K1, P2, K1, P2, K2, P1; rep from * to end.

Large: *K2, P1, K2, P2, K1, P2, K1, P2, (K2, P1) twice; rep from * to end.

Rep rnd 1 for desired cuff length.

Low Country Light Stitch Pattern

PfKb: Purl into front of st and keep on needle; knit into back of st, sl both sts off needle.

RT: K2tog and keep on needle, knit first st and sl both sts off needle.

LT: Sk first st, knit second st tbl and keep on needle, knit first st and sl both sts off needle.

Leg Pattern for All Sizes

(Chart on page 15)

Rnd 1: (RT, P1) 1 (2, 2) times, P1, ssk, YO, K2tog, P2, (RT, P1) 1 (1, 2) times.

Rnds 2 and 4: (K2, P1) 1 (2, 2) times, P1, K1, PfKb, K1, P2, (K2, P1) 1 (1, 2) times.

Rnd 3: (LT, P1) 1 (2, 2) times, P1, ssk, YO, K2tog, P2, (LT, P1) 1 (1, 2) times.

Rep rnds 1–4 for patt.

Instep Pattern for Small (Large)

(Chart on page 15)

Rnd 1: [P] (RT, P1) 1 (2) times, P1, ssk, YO, K2tog, P2, (RT, P1) 1 (2) times.

Rnds 2 and 4: [P] (K2, P1) 1 (2) times, P1, K1, PfKb, K1, P2, (K2, P1) 1 (2) times.

Rnd 3: [P] (LT, P1) 1 (2) times, P1, ssk, YO, K2tog, P2, (LT, P1) 1 (2) times.

Rep rnds 1–4 for patt.

Instep Pattern for Medium

(Chart on page 15)

Rnd 1: K1, P1, RT, P2, ssk, YO, K2tog, P2, RT, P1, K1.

Rnds 2 and 4: K1, P1, K2, P2, K1, PfKb, K1, P2, (K2, P1), K2 2 times.

Rnd 3: K1, P1, LT, P2, ssk, YO, K2tog, P2, LT, P1, K1.

Rep rnds 1–4 for patt.

COLOR TRANSITIONS (CT)

A *Gradiance* yarn set contains four color-coordinated yarns designed to work in a series. At each transition from one color (the old color) to the next (the new color), you'll follow a 12-round sequence, while AT THE SAME TIME working the four-round stitch pattern and any directions for shaping. There will be three stitch-pattern repeats (four rounds each) in each 12-round color transition as follows.

> **First pattern repeat:**
> 1 round new color
> 3 rounds old color
>
> **Second pattern repeat:**
> 2 rounds new color
> 2 rounds old color
>
> **Third pattern repeat:**
> 3 rounds new color
> 1 round old color

There are six color transitions in all, and they are preceded and separated by sections of knitting in one color alone. The one-color sections vary in length according to the size, 1 (1¼, 1½)" in length, not including the heel flap and heel turn. For ease of tracking simultaneous rounds of the stitch pattern and the color transitions, begin all color transitions with round 1 of the stitch pattern.

Cuff

With smaller dpns, and color 4, CO 52 (64, 76) sts. Divide sts evenly on 4 needles; 13 (16, 19) sts per needle. Join, being careful not to twist sts. Work ribbing patt for your size until cuff measures 1 (1¼, 1½)".

Leg

Note that you will be working color transitions (CT) for leg as follows:

CT 1   color 4 (old) to color 3 (new)
Then color 3 alone
CT 2   color 3 (old) to color 2 (new)
Then color 2 alone
CT 3   color 2 (old) to color 1 (new)
Then color 1 alone

Switch to larger dpns, and work rnd 1 of leg patt with color 3; this is rnd 1 of first color transition. When 12-rnd color transition is complete, cont in st patt using color 3 alone until leg length is 3 (3½, 4)". Work a color transition to color 2, and then cont with color 2 alone until leg length is 5 (5¾, 6½)". Work color transition to color 1. When color transition to color 1 is complete, leg should measure approx 6 (6¾, 7½)". Regardless of exact length, it is recommended for ease of working heel to beg heel flap at the end of this color transition.

Heel Flap

The heel is worked with color 1 back and forth in rows on 25 (32, 37) sts, beg with WS row and ending with RS row. To set up heel flap:

For Small (Large): Transfer sts from needle 4 to needle 3 and set empty needle aside. Sl 1 st from needle 3 to needle 1. Sts per needle are (14, 13, 25) for Small and (20, 19, 37) for Large.

For Medium: Knit the first st on needle 1 with needle 4; transfer sts on needle 4 to needle 3 and set empty needle aside. Sl 1 st from needle 3 to needle 2. Sts per needle are (15, 17, 32) for Medium.

For all sizes, heel is worked on needle 3. Turn work and beg on WS row.

Rows 1 and 3: K1, purl to last st, sl 1 wyif.

Row 2: K1, *sl 1 wyib, K1; rep from * to last st, sl 1 wyif.

Row 4: K1, *K1, sl 1 wyib; rep from * to last 2 sts, sl 1 wyib, sl 1 wyif.

Rep rows 1–4 for a total of 26 (32, 38) rows, ending with RS row; Small and Large will end with row 2. There will be 13 (16, 19) slipped sts on each edge.

Heel Turn

The heel turn is worked with color 1.

Row 1 (WS): Sl 1, P13 (17, 19) sts, P2tog, P1, turn.

Row 2: Sl 1, K4 (5, 4), ssk, K1, turn.

Row 3: Sl 1, purl to within 1 st of gap, P2tog (1 st on either side of gap), P1, turn.

Row 4: Sl 1, knit to within 1 st of gap, ssk, K1, turn.

Rep rows 3 and 4, working 1 additional knit or purl st after sl 1 until all side sts are worked, end with RS (knit) row. There are 15 (18, 21) sts left on heel flap.

Cont with color 1 for designated 1 (1¼, 1½)" of gusset and beg next CT; note that gusset may not be complete at this point.

Gusset

For ease of instructions, beg of rnd is now at center bottom of foot. The needles are renumbered at this point and only 3 needles will hold sts for foot; 1 for instep and 2 for sole. Needle 1 is beg of rnd. Sl 8 (9, 11) sts from RH side of heel sts to spare needle you set aside to work heel flap. LH side of heel flap sts are now on needle 1. Cont with needle 1, PU 13 (16, 19) sts from side of heel flap, PU 2 sts at top of gusset (see page 72). Work instep on needle 2 across 27 (32, 39) sts currently on old needles 2 and 3. (Note that for size Medium the first and last sts of instep which were part of a column of RT/LT on leg will be St st on instep.) With new needle 3, PU 2 sts at top of gusset, PU 13 (16, 19) sts from side of heel flap, knit rem 8 (9, 11) heel flap sts onto needle 3. Sts per needle are (22, 27, 23), (27, 32, 27), (31, 39, 32).

Note that as you work the gusset, AT THE SAME TIME, when foot measures 1 (1¼, 1½)" from edge of heel flap, beg color transition from color 1 to color 2.

Gusset Decreases

Needle 1: Knit to last 2 sts, ssk.

Needle 2: Work in established instep patt.

Needle 3: K2tog, knit to end.

Rnd 1:

Needle 1: Knit to last 3 sts, K2tog, K1.

Needle 2: Work in established instep patt.

Needle 3: K1, ssk, knit to end.

Rnd 2:

Needle 1: Knit.

Needle 2: Work in established instep patt.

Needle 3: Knit.

Rep rnds 1 and 2 until 48 (60, 72) total sts rem. Note that there are fewer sts on sole and fewer sts than originally CO. Sts per needle: (10, 27, 11) (14, 32, 14) (16, 39, 17).

Foot

Note that you'll be working color transitions (CT) on foot as follows:

CT 4   color 1 (old) to color 2 (new)
Then color 2 alone
CT 5   color 2 (old) to color 3 (new)
Then color 3 alone
CT 6   color 3 (old) to color 4 (new)
Then color 4 alone

Cont working St st on needles 1 and 3 and established st patt on instep on needle 2.

When foot measures 3 (3½, 4)"
from edge of heel flap, beg color
transition from color 2 to color 3.
When foot measures 5 (5¾, 6½)"
from edge of heel flap, begin color
transition from color 3 to color
4. AT THE SAME TIME, beg toe
shaping after rnd 2 or 4 of st patt
when foot measures 7 (7¾, 8½)" or
desired length from the back of
the heel.

Set-Up Rounds

Rnd 1

Needle 1: Knit.

Needle 2: Knit, dec 6 (4, 6) sts evenly
across needle.

Needle 3: Knit.

Total sts: 44 (56, 68); sts per needle:
(10, 21, 11) (14, 28, 14) (16, 33, 17).

Rnd 2: Knit.

Toe Shaping

Rnd 1

Needle 1: Knit to last 3 sts, K2tog, K1.

Needle 2: K1, ssk, knit to last 3 sts,
K2tog, K1.

Needle 3: K1, ssk knit to end.

Rnd 2: Knit.

Rep rnds 1 and 2 until 28 (32, 40) total
sts rem. Rep rnd 1 only until 16 (16,
20) total sts rem.

With needle 3, knit across sts on
needle 1. Graft toe sts tog using
Kitchener st (see page 73) or
desired grafting method. Weave
in ends.

Leg Pattern for All Sizes

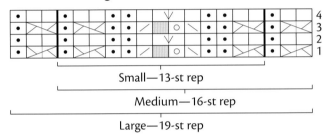

Small—13-st rep

Medium—16-st rep

Large—19-st rep

Note that end-of-rnd st count will vary;
rnds 2 and 4 will be 4 sts more than rnds 1 and 3.

Instep Pattern for Small and Large

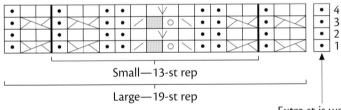

Small—13-st rep

Large—19-st rep

Extra st is worked
only once at beg
of each rnd for
Small and Large.

Instep Pattern for Medium

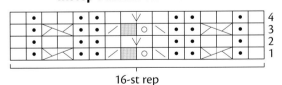

16-st rep

Key

☐ K

• P

⟋ K2tog

⟍ ssk

○ YO

⩗ PfKb: purl into front of st and keep on needle,
knit into back of st, sl both sts off needle

⧓ LT: knit second st on LH needle and keep on
needle, knit first st, sl both sts off needle

⧓ RT: K2tog and keep on needle, knit first st again,
sl both sts off needle

▨ No st

I LOVE GANSEY

Designed by Janine LeCras

♥ **SKILL LEVEL:** Intermediate ■■■□ ♥ **SIZE:** Women's Medium
♥ **FINISHED FOOT CIRCUMFERENCE:** Approx 8" ♥ **SIZING METHOD:** Ⓢ

There is a great history of knitting in the Guernsey islands, and to this day it is possible to buy traditional fishermen's sweaters. The top of the sock mimics the welt of a traditional Guernsey, and the rest of the patterns reflect the Celtic history and traditional gansey patterns of the islands in general. Don't be put off by the apparent complexity of this pattern; once the patterns have been set up, they're very easy to follow.

Materials

1 skein of Foot Prints from The Unique Sheep (100% superwash merino; 4 oz; 305 m/331 yds) in color Aqua Sky (**2**)

Set of 5 double-pointed needles in size 2 (2.75 mm) or size required for gauge

Cable needle

Tapestry needle

Gauge

8 sts = 1" in St st worked in the rnd.

Special Abbreviations

1/1CFP: Sl 1 st to cn and hold at front, P1, K1 from cn.

1/1CBP: Sl 1 st to cn and hold at back, K1, P1 from cn.

1/1CF: Sl 1 st to cn and hold at front, K1, K1 from cn.

1/1CB: Sl 1 st to cn and hold at back, K1, K1 from cn.

Cable A

(Chart on page 18)

(*Worked over 4 sts*)

Row 1: 1/1CF.

Rows 2, 3, and 4: Knit.

Rep rows 1–4 for patt.

Cable B

(Chart on page 18)

(*Worked over 4 sts*)

Row 1: 1/1CB.

Rows 2, 3, and 4: Knit.

Rep rows 1–4 for patt.

Cable C

(Chart on page 18)

(*Worked over 8 sts*)

Rows 1, 2, and 3: K1, P1, K1, P2, K1, P1, K1.

Row 4: K1, P1, 1/1CFP, 1/1CBP, P1, K1.

Row 5: K1, P2, C2F, P2, K1.

Row 6: 1/1CFP, 1/1CBP, 1/1CFP, 1/1CBP.

Row 7: P1, C2B, P2, C2F, P1.

Row 8: 1/1CBP, 1/1CFP, 1/1CBP, 1/1CFP.

Row 9: K1, P2, C2B, P2, K1.

Row 10: K1, P1, 1/1CBP, 1/1CFP, P1, K1.

Rows 11, 12, and 13: K1, P1, K1, P2, K1, P1, K1.

Row 14: K1, P1, 1/1CFP, 1/1CBP, P1, K1.

Row 15: K1, P2, C2B, P2, K1.

Row 16: 1/1CFP, 1/1CBP, 1/1CFP, 1/1CBP.

Row 17: P1, C2B, P2, C2F, P1.

Row 18: 1/1CBP, 1/1CFP, 1/1CBP, 1/1CFP.

Row 19: K1, P2, C2F, P2, K1.

Row 20: K1, P1, 1/1CBP, 1/1CFP, P1, K1.

Rep rows 1–20 for patt.

Gansey Heart Pattern

(Chart on page 18)

(*Worked over 11 sts*)

Rows 1–6: Knit.

Row 7: K3, P1, K3, P1, K3.

Rows 8, 10, and 12: K2, P1, K1, P1, K1, P1, K1, P1, K2.

Rows 9, 11, and 13: K3, P1, K1, P1, K1, P1, K3.

Row 14: K4, P1, K1, P1, K4.

Row 15: K5, P1, K5.

Rep rows 1–15 for patt.

Cuff

CO 64 sts. Divide sts evenly on 4 needles; 16 sts per needle. Join, being careful not to twist sts. Purl 1 rnd, knit 1 rnd. Work 8 rnds in K2, P2 ribbing. Work 5 rows garter st, starting with a purl row. On the last row, dec 2 sts by working P2tog on opposite sides of rnd—62 sts.

Leg

Set-up row: *P2, work row 1 of cable C, P2, work row 1 of cable A, P2, work row 1 of gansey heart patt, P2, work row 1 of cable B; rep from * once to complete the rnd. (For larger sizes work additional purl sts between charts, and for smaller size, work only 1 purl st between charts.)

Work patts as established until 3 reps of cable C have been completed.

Make a note of what rnds you are on in the heart patt and both cable A and cable B so that you will know where you are after you turn the heel when you resume the patt down the instep.

Heel Flap

The heel flap is worked on 31 sts. You can cont patt on heel, or work your favorite heel flap instead.

Work across needle 1 in established patt until you reach middle of cable C. With a new needle knit last 4 sts from cable C and next 27 sts in established patt (which will bring you around to middle of second cable C). Place these sts on waste yarn or a st holder.

Cont heel flap on rem 31 sts and work established patts as follows: Sl 1, K1, P1, K1, P2, cable A, P2, gansey heart patt, P2, cable B, P2, K1, P1, K2. Work back and forth, sl first st of each row, maintaining established patt and remembering to knit the purl sts and purl the knit sts as they face you on the WS rows.

When you have worked one full rep of gansey heart patt, cont center 11 sts in St st until you have worked 15 slipped sts on each side of heel flap.

Heel Turn

Row 1: K19, ssk, K1, turn.

Row 2: Sl 1, P8, P2tog, P1, turn.

Row 3: Sl 1, knit to within 1 st of gap, ssk (1 st on either side of gap), K1, turn.

Row 4: Sl 1, purl to within 1 st of gap, P2tog, P1, turn.

Rep rows 3 and 4, working 1 additional knit or purl st after sl 1 until all heel sts have been worked. There are 19 sts on heel flap.

Gusset

K19 across heel flap; this needle becomes needle 1 below. Renumber needles at this point. Only 3 needles will be used to hold working sts. Instep sts will be on needle 2 and sole sts on needles 1 and 3.

Needle 1: PU 15 sts down edge of heel flap in sl st loops.

Needle 2: Work across 31 instep sts, cont as established in patts as follows: P1, K1, P1, K1, P2, cable A, P2, gansey heart patt, P2, cable B, P2, K1, P1, K1, P1.

Needle 3: PU 15 sts on other side of heel flap and knit across 10 sts of heel—80 sts. Pm at this point to indicate beg of rnd.

Gusset Decrease

Rnd 1

Needle 1: Knit to last 3 sts, K2tog, K1.

Needle 2: Work instep in established patts.

Needle 3: K1, ssk, knit to end.

Rnd 2

Needle 1: Knit.

Needle 2: Work instep in established patts.

Needle 3: Knit.

Rep rnds 1 and 2 until 62 total sts rem.

Foot

Cont St st on needles 1 and 3 and established patts on needle 2 until there are 3 gansey heart patt reps in center panel. Cont center panel in St st until foot measures 7¾", or 2" less than desired length.

Toe Shaping

Rnd 1

Needle 1: Knit to last 3 sts, K2tog, K1.

Needle 2: K1, ssk, knit to last 3 sts, K2tog, K1.

Needle 3: K1, ssk, knit to end.

Rnd 2: Knit.

Rep rnds 1 and 2 until 22 total sts rem (11 sts on needle 2).

Knit across sts on needle 1 with needle 3 (11 sts on needle 3). Graft toe sts tog using Kitchener st (see page 73) or desired grafting method. Weave in ends.

Cable A

Cable B

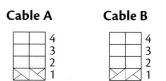

Cable C

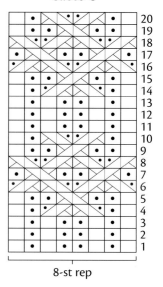

8-st rep

Gansey Heart Pattern

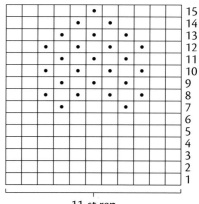

11-st rep

Key

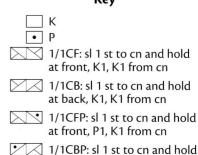

☐ K

• P

1/1CF: sl 1 st to cn and hold at front, K1, K1 from cn

1/1CB: sl 1 st to cn and hold at back, K1, K1 from cn

1/1CFP: sl 1 st to cn and hold at front, P1, K1 from cn

1/1CBP: sl 1 st to cn and hold at back, K1, P1 from cn

♥ **SKILL LEVEL:** Expert ◼◼◼▭ ♥ **SIZE:** Women's Small (Extra Large)
♥ **FINISHED FOOT CIRCUMFERENCE:** Approx 7 (10)" ♥ **SIZING METHOD:** Ⓢ

Aliyya envisioned a romantic sock for Valentine's Day. This extravagantly twisty cabled heart pattern certainly fits the bill. The flirty bobbles on the cuff make this sock exciting enough to be worn alone—who says socks aren't sexy? And thus the name "Blush."

Materials

1 skein of Squooshy Yarn from Zen Yarn Garden (80% superwash merino, 20% nylon; 420 yds) in color Blush ❷

Set of 5 double-pointed needles size 1 (2.25 mm) or size required for gauge

Set of 5 double-pointed needles size 2 (2.75 mm)

Cable needle

Tapestry needle

Gauge

8 sts = 1" in St st worked in the rnd on smaller needles

7 sts = 1" in St st worked in the rnd on larger needles

Twisted Cable Heart Pattern

(Chart on facing page)

(*Worked over 16 sts*)

1/1CFP: Sl 1 st to cn and hold at front, P1, K1 from cn.

1/1CBP: Sl 1 st to cn and hold at back, K1, P1 from cn.

2/1CFP: Sl 2 sts to cn and hold at front, P1, K2 from cn.

1/2CBP: Sl 1 st to cn and hold at back, K2, P1 from cn.

2/2CF: Sl 2 sts to cn and hold at front, K2, K2 from cn.

Rnds 1, 2 and 3 are set-up rows and only worked once.

Rnd 1: P6, K4, P6.

Rnd 2: P6, 2/2CF, P6.

Rnd 3: P6, K4, P6.

Rnds 4–19 are cable patt reps.

Rnd 4: P5, 1/2CBP, 2/1CFP, P5.

Rnd 5: P5, K2, P2, K2, P5.

Rnd 6: P4, 1/2CBP, P2, 2/1CFP, P4.

Rnd 7: (P4, K2) twice, P4.

Rnd 8: P3, 1/2CBP, P4, 2/1CFP, P3.

Rnd 9: P3, K2, P6, K2, P3.

Rnd 10: P2, (1/2CBP) twice, (2/1CFP) twice, P2.

Rnd 11: P2, (K2, P1, K2, P2) twice.

Rnd 12: P1, (1/2CBP) twice, P2, (2/1CFP) twice, P1.

Rnd 13: (P1, K2) twice, P4, (K2, P1) twice.

Rnd 14: P1, K1, 1/1CFP, 2/1CFP, P2, 1/2CBP, 1/1CBP, K1, P1.

Rnd 15: (P1, K1) twice, P1, K2, P2, K2, P1, (K1, P1) twice.

Rnd 16: P1, K1, P1, 1/1CFP, 2/1CFP, 1/2CBP, 1/1CBP, P1, K1, P1.

Rnd 17: P1, K1, P2, K1, P1, K4, P1, K1, P2, K1, P1.

Rnd 18: P1, 1/1CFP, 1/1CBP, P1, 2/2CF, P1, 1/1CFP, 1/1CBP, P1.

Rnd 19: P2, 1/1CFP, P2, K4, P2, 1/1CBP, P2.

Rep rnds 4–19 for cable patt.

Toe

With smaller needles and Turkish CO (see page 71), CO 4 sts on each of two dpns. Knit 1 rnd dividing sts on 4 needles; 2 sts per needle.

Rnd 1: K1, M1, K1, on each of the 4 needles—12 sts total.

Rnd 2

Needle 1: Knit to last 2 sts K1, M1, K1.

Needle 2: K1, M1, knit to end.

Needle 3: Knit to last 2 sts K1, M1, K1.

Needle 4: K1, M1, knit to end—16 sts total.

Choose one of the following toe options.

Rounded Toe: Rep rnd 2 every rnd until there are 9 (10) sts on each needle, and then work rnd 2 every other rnd until there are 18 (20) sts on each needle.

Anatomical Toe: Rep rnd 2 every rnd until there are 10 sts on each needle. Pick one of the increased ends and only inc at this one end every rnd until there are a total of 72 (80) sts. Divide sts on 4 needles, 18 (20) sts per needle. Reverse shaping for other sock.

LONGER FOOT

If you prefer a longer foot, extra length for the sock can be added here at the toe by knitting around to desired length. We were able to complete 4 pattern repeats before starting the heel for a foot length of 9". Your knitting gauge may vary.

Foot

Determine top of sock and work twisted cable heart patt over needles 1 and 2. Work St st over needles 3 and 4 for sole.

TS (twist st): Sk first st on LH needle, knit second st on LH needle and leave on needle, then knit the skipped st and sl both sts off needle.

Rnd 1

Needle 1: K2, P0 (1), work twisted cable heart patt, P0 (1).

Needle 2: TS, P0 (1), work twisted cable heart patt, P0 (1).

Needles 3 and 4: Knit.

Rnd 2: Knit the knit sts and purl the purl sts as they face you, except for rnd 19 of twisted cable heart patt; work this rnd as stated.

Work twisted cable heart patt until 2" less than desired length of foot.

Short-Row Heel

The short-row heel will be worked in St st, back and forth on needles 3 and 4. The sts on needles 1 and 2 will rem on hold until you finish the heel. For each row, you will work 1 less st than row before, turn work without completing rest of row, and make a YO (described below) to start following row.

YO FOR SHORT-ROW HEEL

On RS rows: YO by bringing yarn forward and over top of right-hand needle toward the back, then knit next stitch.

On WS rows: YO by bringing yarn forward from back over top of right-hand needle toward the front, then purl next stitch.

Beg heel on a knit row. Knit sts from needles 3 and 4 onto one needle, turn, work WS YO, purl back across heel sts, turn and work RS YO. The first and last sts of heel should now have a snug little YO attached to them.

Shape heel as follows: On RS, knit to first st with a YO (do NOT work this st or its YO), turn, and make new YO. On WS (purl side), purl to first st with a YO (do NOT work this st or its YO), turn, and make new YO. Cont in this manner until only 11 sts rem in middle without YOs.

Beg widening heel: On RS row, knit to first st with a YO, knit that st, and then untwist its YO by inserting the right needle into back loop and slipping it. Sl it back to left needle and knit it tog with following st. On WS row, YO, purl to first st with a YO, purl that st, and then sl its YO and the following st kw on right needle. Sl them back to left needle and purl them tog through back loop.

Cont as follows: On RS rows, YO, knit to first st with a YO, knit that st, the next 2 loops are YOs that need to be untwisted as above, then K3tog (the 2 YOs and next st), turn. On WS rows, YO, purl to first st with a YO, purl that st, the next 2 loops are YOs, then P3tog tbl (the 2 YOs and next st), turn. Cont until you reach last st on each edge of heel, you will need to work its 2 YOs tog with first instep st on next needle.

This is where you will beg working in the rnd again. Sl first 2 YOs onto resting needle 1, untwisting YOs as you did previously on heel (but only previous WS YOs), K3tog through back loops of these 2 YOs along with first st on needle 3.

Work twisted cable heart patt on needles 1 and 2 (as this will match up continuation of patt) until 1 st rems on needle 4. Sl YOs at end of heel needle 1 onto needle 4. Sl these sts and last st of needle 4 onto tip of a spare needle. Using needle 4, K3tog. Using same spare needle, knit enough sts off heel needles (needles 1 and 2) so that you now have same number of sts you previously had on each needle before starting the heel—18 (20) sts per needle.

Cont in twisted cable heart patt with following changes.

Rnd 1
Needles 1 and 2: TS, P0 (1), work twisted cable patt, P0 (1).

Needle 3: TS, P1 (2), knit to end.

Needle 4: Knit.

Rnd 2
Needles 1 and 2: Work established twisted cable heart patt.

Needles 3 and 4: Knit.

Rep rnds 1 and 2 for another 1" ending on patt rnd 16.

Ankle
Next rnd
Needles 1 and 2: Work rnd 17 of twisted cable heart patt.

Needles 3 and 4: Work rnd 1 of twisted cable heart patt, incorporating TS and extra purl st for larger size.

Next rnd
Needles 1 and 2: Work rnd 18 of twisted cable heart patt.

Needles 3 and 4: Work rnd 2 of twisted cable heart patt.

Next rnd
Needles 1 and 2: Work rnd 19 of twisted cable heart patt.

Needles 3 and 4: Work rnd 3 of twisted cable heart patt.

Now you are ready to work same patt reps of rnds 4–19 on all 4 needles.

Leg
Change to larger needles and work patt reps as follows: TS, P0 (1), work twisted cable heart patt, P0 (1). Note that the ankle may become tight as the cable patt pulls the sts tog. If this happens you have a couple of choices. You can increase the needle size, or at this point make a larger size by adding an extra purl st at each end of the patt rep.

Complete as many twisted cable heart patt reps to desired length.

Cuff
Note that if you are making Small sock, *do not* work decs in cuff.

All needles: TS, P2tog, purl to last 2 sts, P2tog—18 sts on each needle.

Rnd 1: K2, P4, K2, P4, K2, P4.

Rnd 2: TS, P4, TS, P4, TS, P4.

Rep rnds 1 and 2 for 1" or desired length.

Bobble Bind Off
(K1, P1, K1, P1, K1) into next st to inc to 5 sts, turn, K5, turn, P5, turn, K5, turn, P5, turn, K5, sl second, third, fourth and fifth sts over first st to dec to 1 st, turn and sl st to RH needle. K1, sl second st over first, cont to BO 6 sts until you get to next TS and rep bobble BO from * to *. Cont until all sts have been worked and you have 12 bobbles. Weave in ends.

Twisted Cable Heart Pattern

16 sts

Key

☐	K
•	P
	2/2CF: sl 2 sts to cn and hold at front, K2, K2 from cn
	1/1CFP: sl 1 st to cn and hold at front, P1, K1 from cn
	1/1CPB: sl 1 st to cn and hold at back, K1, P1 from cn
	2/1CFP: sl 2 sts to cn and hold at front, P1, K2 from cn
	1/2CBP: sl 1 st to cn and hold at back, K2, P1 from cn

ZIGS AND ZAGS

Designed by Carol Schoenfelder

♥ **SKILL LEVEL:** Expert ◼◼◼▭ ♥ **SIZE:** Child's Large (Women's Small, Women's Large, Women's Extra Large) ♥ **FINISHED FOOT CIRCUMFERENCE:** Approx 7 (7¾, 8½, 9¼)" ♥ **SIZING METHOD:** Ⓢ

The clever construction of this toe-up sock combines a star toe with the simple-to-work Fleegle Heel (toe-up version of the Strong Heel) worked in eye of partridge. Adding additional reverse stockinette to the sides of the Zigs and Zags allows this sock to be made in four sizes, quite an accomplishment for such a large, bold pattern.

Materials

2 skeins of Stroll from Knit Picks (75% superwash wool, 25% nylon; 50 g; 231 yds) in color Shoreline Twist 24033 **1**

2 circular needles (24" long) in size 1 (2.25 mm), or size required for gauge

Cable needle

Tapestry needle

Gauge

8 sts = 1" in St st worked in the rnd

Zigzag Pattern

(Chart on page 24)

LT: Sk first st, knit second st tbl and leave on needle, knit first st and sl both sts off needle.

RT: K2tog and leave on needle, knit first st and sl both sts off needle.

1/1CFP: Sl 1 st to cn and hold at front, P1, K1 from cn.

1/1CBP: Sl 1 st to cn and hold at back, K1, P1 from cn.

Rnd 1: P6 (7, 8, 9), K7, P5 (6, 7, 8), K7, P3 (4, 5, 6).

Rnd 2: P6 (7, 8, 9), RT, K3, 1/1CBP, P5 (6, 7, 8), RT, K3, 1/1CBP, P3 (4, 5, 6).

Rnd 3: P6 (7, 8, 9), K6, P6 (7, 8, 9), K6, P4 (5, 6, 7).

Rnd 4: P5 (6, 7, 8), RT, K3, 1/1CBP, P5 (6, 7, 8), RT, K3, 1/1CBP, P4 (5, 6, 7).

Rnd 5: P5 (6, 7, 8), K6, P6 (7, 8, 9), K6, P5 (6, 7, 8).

Rnd 6: P4 (5, 6, 7), RT, K3, 1/1CBP, P5 (6, 7, 8), RT, K3, 1/1CBP, P5 (6, 7, 8).

Rnd 7: P4 (5, 6, 7), K6, P6 (7, 8, 9), K6, P6 (7, 8, 9).

Rnd 8: P3 (4, 5, 6), RT, K3, RT, P5 (6, 7, 8), RT, K3, RT, P6 (7, 8, 9).

Rnd 9: P3 (4, 5, 6), K7, P5 (6, 7, 8), K7, P6 (7, 8, 9).

Rnd 10: P3 (4, 5, 6), 1/1CFP, K3, LT, P5 (6, 7, 8), 1/1CFP, K3, LT, P6 (7, 8, 9).

Rnd 11: P4 (5, 6, 7), K6, P6 (7, 8, 9), K6, P6 (7, 8, 9).

Rnd 12: P4 (5, 6, 7), 1/1CFP, K3, LT, P5 (6, 7, 8), 1/1CFP, K3, LT, P5 (6, 7, 8).

Rnd 13: P5 (6, 7, 8), K6, P6 (7, 8, 9), K6, P5 (6, 7, 8).

Rnd 14: P5 (6, 7, 8), 1/1CFP, K3, LT, P5 (6, 7, 8), 1/1CFP, K3, LT, P4 (5, 6, 7).

Rnd 15: P6 (7, 8, 9), K6, P6 (7, 8, 9), K6, P4 (5, 6, 7).

Rnd 16: P6 (7, 8, 9), LT, K3, LT, P5 (6, 7, 8), LT, K3, LT, P3 (4, 5, 6).

Rep rnds 1–16 for patt.

Toe

Using 2 circular needles, and Turkish CO (see page 71), CO 7 sts per needle. Join, being careful not to twist sts. Knit 1 rnd.

Rnd 1

Needles 1 and 2: K1f&b, pm, K1f&b, K4, pm, K1f&b—10 sts on each needle.

Rnd 2: Knit.

Rnd 3: Needles 1 and 2: (K1f&b, knit to marker) twice, K1f&b, knit to end of needle—13 sts on each needle.

Rnds 4 and 5: Knit.

Rep rnds 3–5 until you have 22 sts on each needle.

Rnd 15: Needles 1 and 2: (K1f&b, knit to marker) twice, K1f&b, knit to end of needle—25 sts each needle.

Rnds 16 and 17: Knit.

Rep rnds 15–17 another 1 (2, 3, 4) times—28 (31, 34, 37) sts on each needle—56 (62, 68, 74) sts total.

Knit until toe is 3", or desired length.

Foot

Needle 1: Beg one sock with rnd 1 of chart, and second sock with rnd 9 so that socks will be symmetrical rather than identical.

Needle 2: Knit 28 (31, 34, 37) sts.

Gusset

Cont established zigzag patt until sock is about 2½ (2¾, 3, 3¼)" less than the desired foot length—approx when sock reaches highest point of arch.

Rnd 1

Needle 1 (instep): Work in established zigzag patt.

Needle 2 (sole): K1f&b, knit to last 2 sts, K1f&b, K1.

Rnd 2

Needle 1: Work in established zigzag patt.

Needle 2: Knit.

Work rnds 1 and 2 until sole reaches back of heel, or 58 (63, 70, 75) sts on sole needle. Stop in middle of a rnd at end of needle 1 on an even-numbered patt row.

Heel Turn

The heel is worked in eye of partridge.

Row 1: K29, (32, 35, 38), K2, ssk, K1, turn.

Row 2 for Child's Large and Women's Large: (Sl 1, P1) 3 times, P2tog, P1, turn.

Row 2 for Women's Small and Women's Extra Large: (Sl 1, P1) 3 times, sl 1, P2tog, P1, turn.

Row 3: Sl 1, knit to within 1 st of gap, ssk (1 st on either side of gap), K1, turn.

Row 4: *Sl 1, P1; rep from * to within 1 st of gap, P2tog, P1, turn.

Row 5: Sl 1, knit to within 1 st of gap, ssk, K1, turn.

Row 6: Sl 1, P2, *sl 1, P1; rep from * to within 1 st of gap, P2tog, P1 turn.

Place a marker between center 2 sts for Child's Large, or at center st for Women's Small and Women's Extra Large.

Rep rows 3–6 until all but 1 st has been worked, ending with a row 3 or 5. (The unworked st is on other side of needle and will be worked later.)

Sts on needles: Needle 1 has 28 (31, 34, 37) sts, and needle 2 has (29 (32, 35, 38) sts.

Leg

Start working in rnd again. Work established zigzag patt on needle 1. For needle 2, work same patt row as for needle 1, replacing the first P1 with a P2tog—28 (31, 34, 37) sts on needle 2.

Cont in established zigzag patt to desired length, ending with completed row 1 or 9.

For taller socks with wider legs: Make incs every so often by substituting P1f&b for a purl st in middle of side purl blocks (4 incs per inc row), for example, on rnds 16, 32, and 40 of leg.

Cuff

Rnd 1: Knit.

Rnd 2: Purl.

Rnd 3: Knit.

Rnd 4: (P1, K1 tbl) around.

Work rnd 4 until cuff measures 1½" or desired length.

BO loosely and weave in ends.

Zigzag Pattern

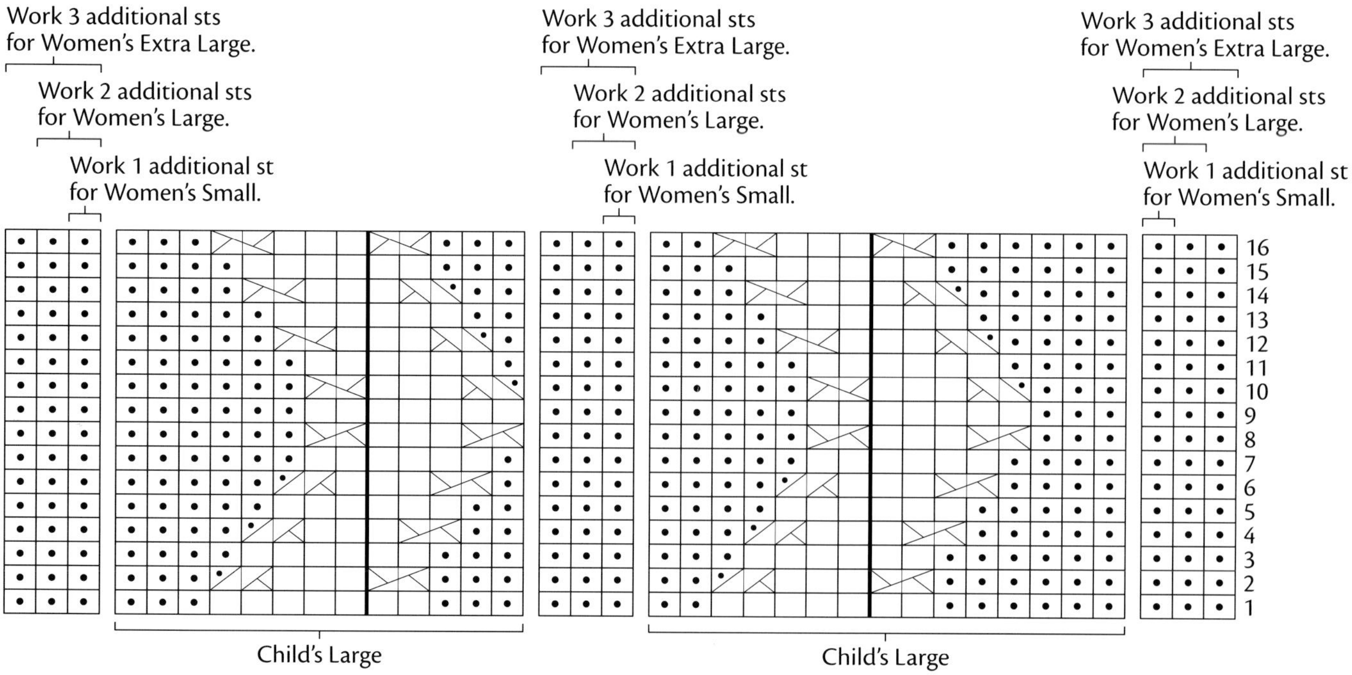

Work 3 additional sts for Women's Extra Large.

Work 2 additional sts for Women's Large.

Work 1 additional st for Women's Small.

Child's Large

Key

☐	K
•	P
⟋⟍	LT: sk first st, knit second st tbl and keep on needle, knit first st, sl both sts off needle
⟍⟋	RT: K2tog and keep on needle, knit first st, sl both sts off needle
⟍⟋	1/1CFP: sl 1 st to cn and hold at front, P1, K1 from cn
•⟋	1/1CPB: sl 1 st to cn and hold at back, K1, P1 from cn

♥ **SKILL LEVEL:** Expert ■■■□ ♥ **SIZES:** Adult's Large
♥ **FINISHED FOOT CIRCUMFERENCE:** Approx 9¼" ♥ **SIZING METHOD:** Ⓑ
*If you change gauge from 7 sts per inch to 8 sts per inch, you get a medium-size sock.

The yarn used for Reina was inspired by Georgia O'Keeffe's painting, Purple Petunia. The instructions for this sock are written for using one long circular needle.

Materials

1 skein of Mama Llama Original Sock 3ply from Mama Llama (100% superwash wool; 460 yds) in hand-painted colorway Georgia's Inspiration (**1**)

1 circular needle (32" or 40") in size 1 (2.25 mm) or size required for gauge

2 stitch markers

Cable needle

Tapestry needle

Gauge

7 sts = 1" in St st worked in the rnd

Special Abbreviation

Wrap 2: Sl 2 sts to cn and hold at front, wrap yarn counterclockwise 3 times around 2 sts on cn, then sl sts to RH needle.

Cuff

CO 64 sts onto 1 circular needle (see page 72). Arrange sts so that 32 sts are on front cable and 32 sts are on back cable. Join into rnd being careful not to twist sts.

Rnds 1 and 2: Purl.

Rnds 3–10: K1, *P2, K2; rep from * to last st, K1.

Rnd 11: K1, *P2, wrap 2, P2, K2; rep from *, end last rep with K1 instead of K2.

Rnds 12–19: As rnds 3–10.

Rnds 20–22: Purl.

Leg

Note that front and back of socks are not the same. Follow written directions below or chart on facing page for front of sock (first 32 sts), beg and ending with K1. Work back of sock (rem 32 sts) in P2, K2 ribbing, beg and ending with K1.

Rnds 1, 3, 5, 7, and 9: For front, K1, P2, K2, P2, K8, P2, K8, P2, K2, P2, K1; for back, K1 *P2, K2; rep from * to last st, K1.

Rnd 2: For front, K1, P2, K2, P2, K1, YO, K1, ssk, K4, P2, K4, K2tog, K1, YO, K1, P2, K2, P2, K1; for back, K1 *P2, K2; rep from * to last st, K1.

Rnd 4: For front, K1, P2, K2, P2, K2, YO, K1, ssk, K3, P2, K3, K2tog, K1, YO, K2, P2, K2, P2, K1; for back, K1, *P2, K2; rep from * to last st, K1.

Rnd 6: For front, K1, P2, K2, P2, K3, YO, K1, ssk, K2, P2, K2, K2tog, K1, YO, K3, P2, K2, P2, K1; for back, K1, *P2, K2; rep from * to last st, K1.

Rnd 8: For front, K1, P2, K2, P2, K4, YO, K1, ssk, K1, P2, K1, K2tog, K1, YO, K4, P2, K2, P2, K1; for back, K1, *P2, K2; rep from * to last st, K1.

Rnd 10: For front, K1, P2, wrap 2, P2, K5, YO, K1, ssk, P2, K2tog, K1, YO, K5, P2, wrap 2, P2, K1; for back, K1, *P2, K2; rep from * to last st, K1.

Rep rnds 1–10.

Work in established patt until leg is desired length.

Knit the first half (front) of rnd 1.

Heel Flap

Heel flap is worked back and forth on back of sock.

Row 1 (RS): *Sl 1, K1; rep from * to end, turn.

Row 2: Sl 1, purl to end, turn.

Rep rows 1 and 2 until you have 16 slipped sts along edge of heel flap, ending after a knit (RS) row; 32 rows worked.

Heel Turn

Row 1: P18, P2tog, P1, turn.

Row 2: Sl 1, K5, K2tog, K1, turn.

Row 3: Sl 1, purl to within 1 st of gap, P2tog (1 st on either side of gap), P1, turn.

Row 4: Sl 1, knit to within 1 st of gap, K2tog, K1, turn.

Rep rows 3 and 4, working 1 additional knit or purl st after sl 1 until all side sts are worked. There are 18 sts on heel flap.

Gusset

PU 17 sts along side of heel flap, pm, knit first 16 sts of chart starting on rnd where you left off before heel turn. On second half of needle, knit second 16 sts of chart, pm, PU 17 sts on other side of heel flap. K9 of rem heel sts so that beg of rnd is now at center of heel. Adjust sts so that you have an equal number on each needle. (The beg of other needle should now be in center of chart and center of instep.)

Gusset Decrease

Maintain instep patt throughout.

Rnd 1: Knit to within 3 sts of marker, K2tog, K1, sm, follow chart to next marker, sm, K1, ssk, knit to end.

Rnd 2: Knit to first marker, sm, follow chart to next marker, sm, knit to end.

Rep rnds 1 and 2 until 64 sts rem.

Foot

Cont established patt on instep and St st on sole sts until foot measures 2" less than desired length. Knit to first marker and adjust your sts on needles so that this (side of foot) is now beg of rnd and you have 32 sts on each needle.

Toe Shaping

Rnd 1: K1, ssk, knit to last 3 sts, K2tog, K1; rep for second half of sts.

Rnd 2: Knit.

Rep rnds 1 and 2 until 12 sts rem on each needle. Graft toe sts tog using Kitchener st (see page 73) or desired grafting method. Weave in ends.

Chart for Leg Front *Only*

32 sts

Key

☐	K
•	P
╱	K2tog
╲	ssk
○	YO
W	Wrap 2: sl 2 sts to cn and hold at front, wrap yarn counterclockwise 3 times around 2 sts on cn, sl sts to RH needle

GOTHIC TEMPTRESS

Designed by Janine Le Cras

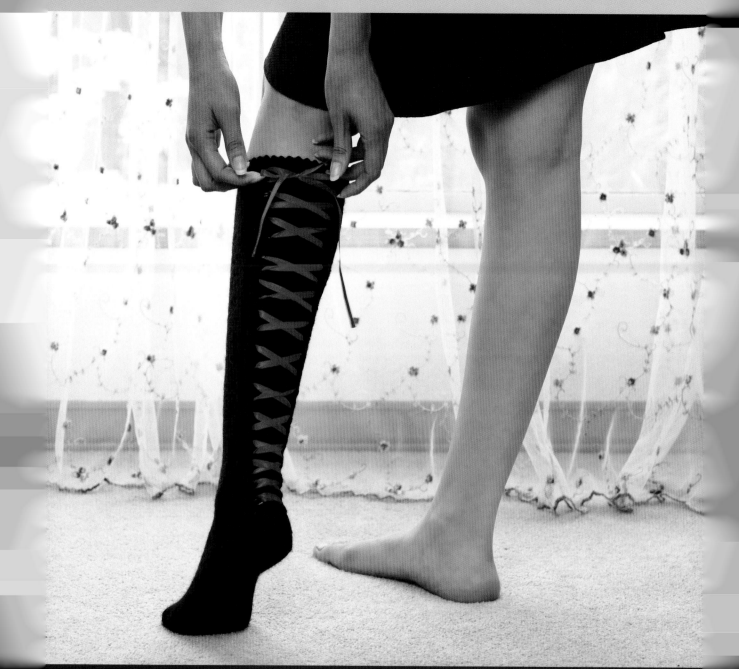

♥ **SKILL LEVEL:** Intermediate ■■■◻ ♥ **SIZES:** Women's Small (Medium, Large)
♥ **FINISHED FOOT CIRCUMFERENCE:** Approx 7½ (8¼, 9)" ♥ **SIZING METHOD:** Ⓑ

This sock was designed for the Scary Sock KAL (knit-along) on Ravelry. All of the designs were inspired by old horror films, and this one is homage to all those gothic ladies out there. Elvira, Morticia, Vampira: This one is for you.

Materials

2 skeins of Classics Courtelle 4 Ply* by Wendy/Peter Pan (100% acrylic; 100g; 426 yds/390 m) in color Raven

Set of 5 double-pointed needles in size 2 (2.75 mm) or size required for gauge

OR 2 circular needles (24" long) in size 2 (2.75 mm) or size required for gauge

Stitch marker

6 yards ¼"-wide satin ribbon, to match or contrast with your yarn, for laces

Cable needle

Tapestry needle

*This yarn is only available in the UK. Substitute any acrylic, superwash wool, or blend with similar yardage and gauge.

Gauge

8 sts = 1" in St st worked in the rnd

Cable Pattern

(Chart at right)

(Worked over 12 sts)

2/2CB: Sl 2 sts to cn and hold at back, K2, K2 from cn.

2/2CF: Sl 2 sts to cn and hold at front, K2, K2 from cn.

Rnd 1: P4, K4, P4.

Rnd 2: P2, 2/2CB, 2/2CF, P2.

Rnds 3, 4, and 5: P2, K2, P4, K2, P2.

Rnd 6: P2, 2/2CF, 2/2CB, P2.

Rnds 7 and 8: P4, K4, P4.

Rep rnds 1–8.

Toe

Using 1 circular needle or 1 dpn, CO 10 sts for all sizes. Knit 1 row. Using another circular needle or dpn, PU 10 sts along CO edge. You should have 2 needles, parallel to each other, with 10 sts on each. Pm to indicate beg of rnd.

Rnd 1: Needles 1 and 2: K1, K1f&b, knit to last 2 sts, K1f&b, K1.

Rnd 2: Knit.

Rep rnds 1 and 2 until there are 64 (68, 72) sts total. If using circular needles, leave as is.

If using dpns, divide sts on 4 dpns so that you have 16 (17, 18) sts on each

needle. You may choose to divide the sts earlier if working with only 2 dpns becomes awkward.

Foot

Cont in St st until the foot measures 7 (7¾, 8¼)" or 2" less than desired length.

Short-Row Heel

If using circular needles, sts on needle just completed will be heel sts. If using dpns, sl last 32 (34, 36), sts onto one needle for heel sts. Place rem sts either on spare needles or st holders until they are needed. Cont in St st on these 32 (34, 36) sts, working back and forth in rows as follows.

Row 1: Knit to last st, w&t.

Row 2: Purl to last st, w&t.

Row 3: Knit to 1 st before wrapped st, w&t.

Row 4: Purl to 1 st before wrapped st, w&t.

Rep rows 3 and 4, working 1 less st at each end of needle until there are 12 unworked sts in middle of needle. All heel sts (32, 34, 36) should still be on needle.

Row 5: Knit to first wrapped st, knit st and wrap tog, turn.

Row 6: Purl to first wrapped st, purl st and wrap tog, turn.

Row 7: Knit to next wrapped st, knit st and wrap tog, turn.

Row 8: Purl to next wrapped st, purl st and wrap tog, turn.

Rep rows 7 and 8, working 1 more st at each end of needle until wrapped sts and their wraps have been worked. A total of (32, 34, 36) sts should still be on the needle.

Leg

Set-up row for corset cables. If using dpns, divide heel sts on 2 needles, 16 (17, 18) sts each.

Heel needles: K2, (3, 4) work row 1 of cable chart, P4, work row 1 of cable chart, K2 (3, 4).

Instep needle(s): Knit all sts.

Resume working in rnd, working right to left on all rows of cable chart. AT THE SAME TIME when leg measures 3", beg calf shaping by making a pair of lifted incs between cable repeats

as follows: Work across first cable rep, lift bar between last st of first cable and first purl st, purl into back of st. Work to bar between last purl st and first st of second cable rep, lift bar and purl into back of st. Rep incs every 18th rnd until you have made 6 (7, 8) total sets of paired incs.

Cont without shaping until cuff measures desired length. The beauty of toe-up socks is that you can try them on as you go to check how they fit and determine desired length accurately. If you wish to make these socks as thigh-highs, you can add more incs once you pass the knee.

Picot Edging

Rnds 1–8: Knit.

Rnd 9: K2tog, YO.

Rnds 10–17: Knit.

BO all sts loosely.

Finishing

Fold over top of sock so picot edging is at edge and sl st hem in place—be sure not to st too tightly or sock top will be too tight. If you find the sock slips down, thread a length of ¼"-wide elastic through the picot edging.

Weave in ends. Block socks using your preferred method. Cut satin ribbon into 2 equal lengths and thread through the centers of cables from top to bottom and back. Finish with a neat bow at top. Trim any excess ribbon on the bias to prevent fraying.

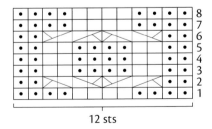

Cable Pattern

12 sts

Key

☐ K

⊡ P

2/2CF: sl 2 sts to cn and hold at front, K2, K2 from cn

2/2CB: sl 2 sts to cn and hold at back, K2, K2 from cn

CELTIC SPIRIT

Designed by Judy Alexander

♥ **SKILL LEVEL:** Expert ◖█◗◖█◗◖█◗◻◻ ♥ **SIZES:** Adult's Medium (Large)
♥ **FINISHED FOOT CIRCUMFERENCE:** Approx 8 (9)" ♥ **SIZING METHOD:** Ⓑ

A conjunction of several elements brought about this sock design. Judy was beginning to work on a St. Patrick's Day sock for TheKnitter.com March kit, when she received a new color card from Misti Alpaca in this lovely green. She'd always loved the Clustered Braid Cable from Barbara Walker's A Second Treasury of Knitting Patterns, and the color-and-pattern combination seemed perfect for TheKnitter.com March design.

Materials

2 skeins of Misti Alpaca Lace from Misti International, Inc. (100% baby alpaca; 50 g; 437 yds) in color Green Meadow 8501 [1]

(*Sock is worked with 2 strands of yarn held tog throughout.*)

Set of 5 double-pointed needles in size 1 (2.25 mm) or size required for gauge

Cable needle

Tapestry needle

Gauge

8 sts = 1" in St st worked in the rnd with 2 strands of yarn held tog

Twisted Ribbing

RT: Knit second st on LH needle, knit into first st on LH needle and slip both sts off needle.

Rnd 1: *P2, RT; rep from *.

Rnd 2: *P2, K2; rep from *.

Rep rnds 1 and 2.

Celtic Cable Pattern

(Chart on page 32)

(*Worked over 28 sts*)

2/2CF: Sl 2 sts to cn and hold at front, K2, K2 from cn.

2/2CB: Sl 2 sts to cn and hold at back, K2, K2 from cn.

2/1CFP: Sl 2 sts to cn and hold at front, P1, K2 from cn.

1/2CBP: Sl 1 st to cn and hold at back, K2, P1 from cn.

Cluster 6: K2, P2, K2, then sl last 6 sts worked to cn, wrap yarn counterclockwise 4 times around 6 sts, sl sts back to RH needle.

Rnds 1, 3, 17, and 19: K4, (P4, K4) 3 times.

Rnds 2 and 18: C4F, P4, C4B, P4, C4F, P4, C4F.

Rnds 4 and 20: K4, P3, 1/2CBP, 2/1CFP, P2, 1/2CBP, 2/1CFP, P3, K4.

Rnds 5, 15, 21, and 23: K4, P3, (K2, P2) 3 times, K2, P3, K4.

Rnd 6: C4F, P2, 1/2CBP, P2, 2/1CFP, 1/2CBP, P2, 2/1CFP, P2, C4F.

Rnds 7, 9, 11, and 13: K4, P2, K2, P4, K4, P4, K2, P2, K4.

Rnds 8 and 12: K4, P2, K2, P4, C4B, P4, K2, P2, K4.

Rnd 10: C4F, P2, K2, P4, K4, P4, K2, P2, C4F.

Rnd 14: C4F, P2, 2/1CFP, P2, 1/2CBP, 2/1CFP, P2, 1/2CBP, P2, C4F.

Rnd 16: K4, P3, 2/1CFP, 1/2CBP, P2, 2/1CFP, 1/2CBP, P3, K4.

Rnd 22: C4F, P3, K2, P2, cluster 6, P2, K2, P3, C4F.

Rnd 24: K4, P3, 2/1CFP, 1/2CBP, P2, 2/1CFP, 1/2CBP, P3, K4.

Rep rnds 1–24 for patt.

Cuff and Leg

With 2 strands of yarn held tog, CO 66 (74) sts. Distribute sts on 4 needles as follows: (20, 14, 14, 18), (24, 14, 14, 22). Join, being careful to not twist sts. Set up patt as follows.

For Medium: (K2, P2) 5 times, (K4, P4) 3 times, K4, (P2, K2) 4 times, P2.

For Large: (K2, P2) 6 times, (K4, P4) 3 times, K4, (P2, K2) 5 times, P2.

Rnd 1: For both sizes, on next rnd, work 20 (24) sts in K2, P2 ribbing, work rnd 1 of Celtic cable on next 28 sts (needles 2 and 3), finish rnd in K2, P2 ribbing.

Rnds 2–9: Cont in established K2, P2 ribbing and Celtic cable patt.

Rnd 10: Cont in established patt, switching from K2, P2 ribbing to twisted ribbing.

Cont as established until sock measures 8" or desired length from beg of cuff.

Heel Flap

This sock has a Dutch heel.

Heel flap is started over center 34 (38) sts of twisted ribbing on needles 1 and 4. The Celtic cable patt is centered on instep needles (2 and 3). Move 2 (4) sts from needle 1 to needle 2, then move 2 (4) sts from needle 4 to needle 3—sts per needle: (18, 16, 16, 16), (20, 18, 18, 18). The instep is worked over 32 (36) sts, with 2 (4) sts worked in twisted ribbing on each side of Celtic cable patt. Combine sts on needle 1 and 4 to one needle to work heel flap. Center sts for heel flap so that it beg and ends with a RT (P2). Beg on WS row.

Row 1: K3, inc 1, purl to last 3 sts, K3—35 (39) sts for heel flap.

Row 2: K3, (sl 1, K1) to last 4 sts, sl 1, K3.

Row 3: K3, purl to last 3 sts, K3.

Rep rows 2 and 3 until heel flap measures 2½".

Heel Turn

Row 1: K23 (25), ssk, turn.

Row 2: Sl 1, P11 (12), P2tog, turn.

Row 3: Sl 1, K11 (12), ssk, turn.

Rep rows 2 and 3 until all sts are used and there are 13 (14) sts on needle. End with completed WS row.

Gusset

For Medium: Knit first 5 sts, K2tog. Rnd now starts in middle of heel flap.

For Large: Knit first 7 sts. Rnd now starts in middle of heel flap.

For both sizes: With needle 1, K6 (7), PU 1 st at edge of each garter ridge along heel flap. Work Celtic cable patt across instep needles 2 and 3. With needle 4, PU 1 st at edge of each garter ridge along other side of heel flap, work rem 6 (7) sts.

Work 1 rnd in established Celtic cable patt on instep sts, and in St st on sole sts.

Gusset Decrease

Rnd 1

Needle 1: Knit to last 2 sts, K2tog.

Needles 2 and 3: Work instep in established patt.

Needle 4: Ssk, knit to end.

Rnds 2 and 3

Needle 1: Knit.

Needles 2 and 3: Work instep in established patt.

Needle 4: Knit.

Rep rnds 1–3 until 64 (72) total sts rem.

Foot

Cont with established patt on instep sts and St st on sole sts until foot is 2" less than desired length. End with row 4, 16, or 24 of Celtic cable patt.

Toe Shaping

Dec Rnd

Needle 1: Knit to last 3 sts, K2tog, K1.

Needle 2: K1, ssk, knit to end.

Needle 3: Knit to last 3 sts, K2tog, K1.

Needle 4: K1, ssk, knit to end.

Knit 3 rnds.

Work (dec rnd, knit 2 rnds) twice.

Work (dec rnd, knit 1 rnd) 3 times.

Work dec rnd until 8 total sts rem on needles. Graft sts tog using Kitchener st (see page 73) or desired grafting method. Weave in ends.

Celtic Cable Pattern

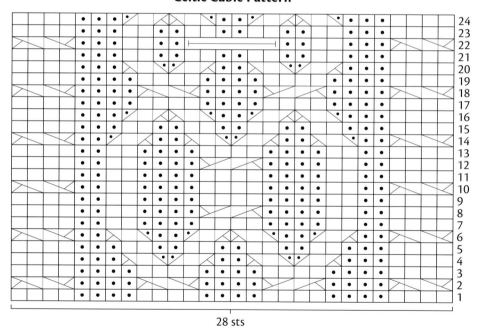

28 sts

Key

◻ K

• P

2/2CF: sl 2 sts to cn and hold at front, K2, K2 from cn

2/2CB: sl 2 sts to cn and hold at back, K2, K2 from cn

2/1CFP: sl 2 sts to cn and hold at front, P1, K2 from cn

1/2CBP: sl 1 st to cn and hold at back, K2, P1 from cn

Cluster 6: K2, P2, K2, sl last 6 sts to cn, wrap yarn counterclockwise 4 times around 6 sts, sl sts back to RH needle

♥ **SKILL LEVEL:** Intermediate ◼◼◼◻ ♥ **SIZES:** Women's Small (Medium, Large)
♥ **FINISHED FOOT CIRCUMFERENCE:** Approx 7 (8, 9)" ♥ **SIZING METHOD:** Ⓝ

The striking yarn used in these socks is hand dyed using a sock blank (a machine-knit rectangle) knit with two strands of undyed yarn. The color gradually shifts from orange at one end to brown at the other. The two strands are separated and each then wound into a separate ball: each sock is knit using both ends of one ball alternately. To substitute yarns that are not dyed in this manner, you could use 2 balls of yarn in complementary colors worked alternately.

Materials

1 skein of Squishy Sock Yarn from Knit it Up; Kate McMullin, dyer (75% superwash wool, 25% nylon; 100 g; 460 yds) in color Dr. Jones 2

One set of 5 double-pointed needles in size 2 (2.75 mm) or size required for gauge

One set of 5 double-pointed needles in size 1 (2.25 mm) or size required for gauge

1 stitch marker

Tapestry needle

Gauge

9 sts and 10 rnds = 1" in tweed sl st patt worked in the rnd on larger needles

Tweed Slip Stitch Pattern

Pattern is worked using both ends of ball. All sl sts are slipped as if to purl wyib.

Rnd 1: With brown, *K1, sl 1; rep from * to end.

Rnd 2: With brown, knit.

Rnd 3: With orange, *K1, sl 1; rep from * to end.

Rnd 4: With orange, knit.

Rnd 5: With brown, *sl 1, K1; rep from * to end.

Rnd 6: With brown, knit.

Rnd 7: With orange, *sl 1, K1; rep from * to end.

Rnd 8: With orange, knit.

Rep rnds 1–8.

Cuff

Using smaller dpn and orange end of yarn, CO 64 (72, 80) sts. Divide sts evenly on 4 smaller dpns; 16 (18, 20) sts per needle. Join, being careful not to twist sts, pm to designate beg of rnd if desired. Work P1, K1 ribbing until cuff measures 1 (1¼, 1½)".

Leg

Change to larger dpns and join brown end of yarn. Work tweed sl st patt, twisting new and old strands every time you change color (beg of every odd-numbered strand; beg of every odd-numbered rnd). Work in patt until leg measures 6¼ (6¾, 7¼)" from top of cuff, ending with rnd 4.

Heel Flap

Change to smaller dpns. Heel flap will be worked back and forth in rows.

Row 1: With brown, *sl 1, K1; rep from * 15 (17, 19) more times, turn.

Row 2: With brown, sl 1, P31 (35, 39), turn.

Row 3: With orange, *sl 1, K1; rep from * 15 (17, 19) more times, turn.

Row 4: With orange, sl 1, P31 (35, 39), turn.

Row 5: With brown, sl 1, K2, *sl 1, K1; rep from * to last 2 sts, K2, turn.

Row 6: With brown, sl 1, P31 (35, 39), turn.

Row 7: With orange, sl 1, K2, *sl 1, K1; rep from * to last 2 sts, K2, turn.

Row 8: With orange, sl 1, P31 (35, 39), turn.

For Small and Medium: Rep rows 1–8 once more, then rep rows 1–7 once.

For Large: Rep rows 1–8 two more times, then rep rows 1–3 once.

For all sizes: Cut brown yarn.

Heel Turn

Heel will be turned solely with orange yarn.

Row 1: Sl 1, P16 (18, 20), P2tog, P1, turn.

Row 2: Sl 1, K3, ssk, K1, turn.

Row 3: Sl 1, purl to within 1 st of gap, P2tog (1 st on either side of gap), P1, turn.

Row 4: Sl 1, knit to within 1 st of gap, ssk, K1, turn.

Rep rows 3 and 4, working 1 additional knit or purl st after sl 1 until 2 sts rem on each side.

Next row: Sl 1, purl to within 1 st of gap, P2tog, P1, turn.

Next row: Sl 1, knit to within 1 st of gap, K2tog, K1. Do not turn work. There are 20 (22, 24) sts on heel flap.

Rejoin brown yarn and resume working in rnd. For ease of working, beg of instep is now beg of rnd. Needles 1 and 2 will hold instep sts, and needles 3 and 4 will hold gusset and sole sts. The needle currently holding heel sts is needle 4.

With needle 4, PU 12 (14, 16) sts up side of heel flap. With needles 1 and 2, work 32 (36, 40) instep sts as rnd 5 of tweed sl st patt. With needle 3, PU 12 (14, 16) sts down side of heel flap and knit across first 10 (11, 12) sts of heel—76 (86, 96) total sts. On needle 4, K10 (11, 12) sts in brown, then *K1 with orange, K1 with brown; rep from * 5 (6, 7) more times. Pm for new beg of rnd.

Gusset

Switch back to larger dpns.

Throughout gusset shaping, work tweed sl st patt on needles 1 and 2 starting with rnd 6. Work sts on needle 3 and 4 as follows, while cont to alternate 2 rnds of brown and 2 rnds of orange.

Rnd 1 (in brown)

Needles 1 and 2: Work tweed sl-st patt as established.

Needle 3: Ssk, knit to end.

Needle 4: Knit to last 2 sts, K2tog.

Rnd 2 (in orange)

Needles 1 and 2: Work tweed sl-st patt as established.

Needles 3 and 4:

For Small and Large: *Sl 1, K1; rep from * to end.

For Medium: Work rnd 7 of tweed sl-st patt.

Rnd 3 (in orange)

Needles 1 and 2: Work tweed sl-st patt as established.

Needle 3: Ssk, knit to end.

Needle 4: Knit to last 2 sts, K2tog.

Rnd 4 (in brown)

Needles 1 and 2: Work tweed sl-st patt as established.

Needles 3 and 4:

For Small and Large: Work rnd 1 of tweed sl-st patt.

For Medium: Beg at needle 3, *sl 1, K1; rep from * to end.

Rnd 5: As rnd 1.

Rnd 6

Needles 1 and 2: Work tweed sl-st patt as established.

Needles 3 and 4:

For Small and Large: Beg at needle 3, *sl 1, K1; rep from * to end.

For Medium: Work rnd 3 of tweed sl-st patt.

Rnd 7: As rnd 3.

Rnd 8

Needles 1 and 2: Work tweed sl-st patt as established.

Needles 3 and 4:

For Small and Large: Work rnd 5 of tweed sl-st patt.

For Medium: Beg at needle 3, *K1, sl 1; rep from * to end.

Rnd 9: As rnd 1.

Rnd 10

Needles 1 and 2: Work tweed sl-st patt as established.

Needles 3 and 4:

For Small and Large: Beg at needle 3, *K1, sl 1; rep from * to end.

For Medium: Work rnd 7 of tweed sl-st patt.

Rnd 11: As rnd 3.

Rnd 12

Needles 1 and 2: Work tweed sl-st patt as established.

Needles 3 and 4:

For Small and Large: Work rnd 1 of tweed sl-st patt.

For Medium: Beg at needle 3, *sl 1, K1; rep from * to end.

Note that small gusset dec should be complete (64 total sts). Skip to instructions for foot.

Rnd 13: As rnd 1.

Rnd 14

Needles 1 and 2: Work tweed sl-st patt as established.

Needles 3 and 4:

For Large: Beg at needle 3, *sl 1, K1; rep from * to end.

For Medium: Work rnd 3 of tweed sl-st patt.

Note that Medium gusset dec should be complete (72 total sts). Skip to instructions for foot.

Rnd 15 (for Large only): As rnd 3.

Rnd 16 (for Large only)

Needles 1 and 2: Work tweed sl-st patt as established.

Needles 3 and 4: Work rnd 5 of tweed sl-st patt.

Note that Large gusset dec should be complete (80 total sts). Beg foot.

Foot

Cont in established tweed sl-st patt, which should progress uninterrupted around the sock, until foot measures 7 (7¾, 8¼)" from back of heel, or 1¼" short of desired length.

Toe Shaping

Cut brown yarn and switch to smaller dpns.

Rnd 1

Needles 1 and 3: Ssk, knit to end.

Needles 2 and 4: Knit to last 2 sts, K2tog.

Rnd 2: Knit.

Rep rnds 1 and 2 another five times.

Rep rnd 1 only for next 3 (5, 7) rnds—7 sts rem on each needle 28 sts total.

Finishing

Combine sts on needles 1 and 2 onto one needle. Combine sts on needles 3 and 4 onto another needle. Graft toe sts tog using Kitchener st (see page 73) or desired grafting method. Weave in ends.

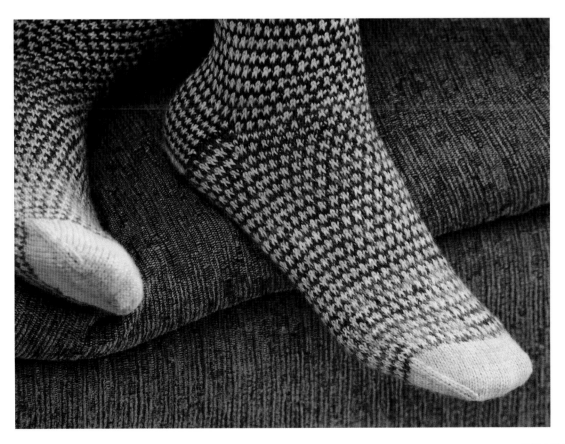

BEADED LATTICE

Designed by Terry Liann Morris

♥ **SKILL LEVEL:** Expert ◖◼◼◼◗ ♥ **SIZES:** Women's Medium (Large)
♥ **FINISHED FOOT CIRCUMFERENCE:** Approx 8 (9)" ♥ **SIZING METHOD:** Ⓝ

Tiny one-by-one crosses and seed beads, matching or contrasting, accent the leg of this pretty sock. The lattice pattern continues down the instep without the beads for greater comfort. This one is knit in a luscious, hand-dyed semi-solid-colored yarn, and the tiny beads reflect the subtly different colors of the yarn.

Materials

1 skein of Hand Dyed Sock! Yarn from Lisa Souza Knitwear and Dyeworks (75% superwash wool, 15% nylon; 113 g; 450 yds/412 m) in color Pumpkin **2**

Set of 5 double-pointed needles in size 1 (2.25 mm) or size required for gauge

112 (126) small seed beads*

Cable needle

Big Eye beading needle

Tapestry needle

This number of beads is for a 6" leg length including cuff. For a longer leg, add 16 (18) additional beads for each patt rep (approx ¾"). If you do, make a note of the number of reps you plan to do.

Gauge

8 sts = 1" in St st worked in the rnd

Special Abbreviations

1/1CF: Sl 1 st to cn and hold at front, K1, K1 from cn.

1/1CB: Sl 1 st to cn and hold at back, K1, K1 from cn.

Sl bead: Sl bead into place.

Beaded Lattice Leg Pattern

(Chart on page 38)

(*Multiple of 8 sts*)

Rnd 1: Knit.
Rnd 2: (K4, 1/1CF, 1/1CB) 8 (9) times.
Rnd 3: (K6, sl bead, K2) 8 (9) times.
Rnd 4: (K4, 1/1CB, 1/1CF) 8 (9) times.
Rnd 5: Knit.
Rnd 6: (1/1CF, 1/1CB, K4) 8 (9) times.
Rnd 7: (K2, sl bead, K6) 8 (9) times.
Rnd 8: (1/1CB, 1/1CF, K4) 8 (9) times.
Rep rnds 1–8 for patt.

Lattice Instep Pattern

(Chart on page 38)

(*Multiple of 10 [14] sts + 2 [6] sts*)

Rnd 1 and all odd-numbered rnds: Knit.
Rnd 2: K1 (3), *(K4, 1/1CF, 1/1CB); rep from * 4 times, K1 (3).
Rnd 4: K1 (3), *(K4, 1/1CB, 1/1CF); rep from * 4 times, K1 (3).

Rnd 6: K1 (3), *(1/1CF, 1/1CB, K4); rep from * 4 times, K1 (3).
Rnd 8: K1 (3), *(1/1CB, 1/1CF, K4); rep from * 4 times, K1 (3).
Rep rnds 1–8 for patt.

Cuff

Using Big Eye needle, string 112 (126) beads (or number calculated for your leg length above), onto your yarn. Count carefully! As you knit, you will slide beads along yarn, using 1 bead at a time, until they are gone.

CO 64 (72) sts. Distribute sts on 4 needles as follows: (16, 16, 16, 16) (16, 24, 16, 16). Join, taking care not to twist sts. (Irregular distribution of sts for Large size is to avoid splitting patt rep.) Work (P1, K2, P1) ribbing for 1½".

Leg

Work beaded lattice leg patt for 7 total vertical reps, or total number of reps determined when stringing your beads for desired length.

Heel Flap

The heel flap is worked back and forth in rows; instep sts will be used later.

Set up for heel flap.

K15 (17), for Medium, sl rem st to needle 1; for Large, K1 st from needle 2, turn.

Sl 1, P14 (16) to center back of sock, P15 (17) sts, for Medium sl rem st to needle 3; for Large K1 from needle 3—30 (34) sts for heel flap.

Divide rem 34 (38) sts evenly between needles 2 and 3 for instep. Set extra needle aside.

Eye of Partridge Heel Pattern

Row 1: *Sl 1, K1; rep from * to end.
Row 2: Sl 1, purl to end.
Row 3: Sl 1, K2, *sl 1, K1; rep from * to end.
Row 4: Sl 1, purl to end.
Rep rows 1–4 until heel flap measures 2 (2¼)". End with row 2 or row 4.

Heel Turn

Row 1: Sl 1, K16 (18), ssk, K1, turn. There will be 10 (12) unworked sts.
Row 2: Sl 1, P5, P2tog, P1, turn.
Row 3: Sl 1, knit to within 1 st of gap, ssk (1 st on either side of gap), K1, turn.
Row 4: Sl 1, purl to within 1 st of gap, P2tog, P1, turn.
Rep rows 3 and 4, working 1 additional knit or purl st after sl 1 until all side sts are worked, end with a WS (purl row). There are 18 (20) sts on heel flap.

Next row: Sl 1, knit to end.

Gusset

Work lattice instep patt without beads. With heel flap needle (needle 1), PU 15 (17) sts along edge of heel flap. With needle set aside earlier, work lattice instep patt across both instep needles onto needle 2. With needle 3, PU 15 (17) sts along rem heel flap edge, then K9 (10) sts from needle 1. This is center of sole and beg of rnd. There are 82 (92) total sts. Sts per needle: (24, 34, 24) (27, 38, 27).

Gusset Decrease

Rnd 1
Needle 1: Knit to last 3 sts, K2tog, K1.
Needle 2: Work in established instep patt.
Needle 3: K1, ssk, knit to end.

Rnd 2
Needle 1: Knit.
Needle 2: Work in established instep patt.
Needle 3: Knit.

Rep rnds 1 and 2 until 64 (72) total sts rem; sts per needle (15, 34, 15) (17, 38, 17).

Foot

Cont working in St st on needles 1 and 3 and established instep patt on needle 2 until foot measures 7 (8)" from back of heel or 2" less than desired length; end with rnd 4 or rnd 8.

Rearrange sts for toe by slipping first st from needle 2 to needle 1, and sl last st from needle 2 to needle 3. Sts per needle: (16, 32 16) (18, 36, 18).

Toe Shaping

Rnd 1

Needle 1: Knit to the last 3 sts, K2tog, K1.

Needle 2: K1, ssk, knit to the last 3 sts, K2tog, K1.

Needle 3: K1, ssk, knit to end.

Rnd 2: Knit.

Rnd 3: Knit.

Rep rnds 1–3 once. Rep rnds 1 and 2 only until 36 sts rem. Rep rnd 1 only until 24 sts rem. With needle 3, knit sts on needle 1. Graft toe sts tog using Kitchener st (see page 73) or desired grafting method. Weave in ends.

Beaded Lattice Leg Pattern

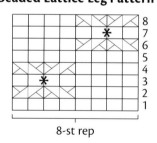

8-st rep

Key

	K
⊠	1/1CF: sl 1 st to cn and hold at front, K1, K1 from cn
⊠	1/1CB: sl 1 st to cn and hold at back, K1, K1 from cn
✱	sl bead

Lattice Instep Pattern

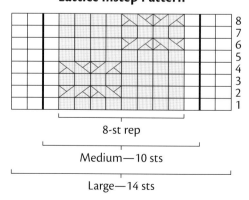

8-st rep

Medium—10 sts

Large—14 sts

ARIEL

Designed by Debbie O'Neill

♥ **SKILL LEVEL:** Expert ◼◼◼◻ ♥ **SIZES:** Women's Medium (Extra Large)
♥ **FINISHED FOOT CIRCUMFERENCE:** Approx 8 (10)" ♥ **SIZING METHOD:** Ⓝ Ⓖ

The lace motif in this sock is based on a Japanese stitch pattern that is reminiscent of mermaid tails—hence the name Ariel! It's a large motif that makes a striking sock. Knit with a lycra blend, these socks feel snug and warm.

Materials

2 skeins of Soxx Appeal from Knit One Crochet Two (96% superwash merino wool, 3% nylon, 1% elastic; 50 g; 208 yds/190 m) in color Teal 9553 **2**

Set of 4 double-pointed needles in size 1 (2.25 mm) or size required for gauge

Tapestry needle

Gauge

8 sts =1" in St st worked in the rnd

NOTE ON SIZING

The lace repeat in this sock is quite large, so there is a significant difference between the Small and Large size. However, the yarn used is very elastic, so the sizes as written will fit a wide variety of feet. If you wish to further vary the sizing, try going up or down a needle size as needed.

Mermaid Tail Lace Pattern

(Chart on facing page)

(*Multiple of 16 sts*)

Rnd 1: *YO, K3, ssk, K2tog, YO, P1, YO, ssk, K2tog, K3, YO, P1; rep from *.

Rnd 2: *K1, YO, K2, ssk, K2, P1, K2, K2tog, K2, YO, K1, P1; rep from *.

Rnd 3: *K2, YO, K1, ssk, YO, ssk, P1, K2tog, YO, K2tog, K1, YO, K2, P1; rep from *.

Rnd 4: *K3, YO, ssk, K2, P1, K2, K2tog, YO, K3, P1; rep from *.

Rnd 5: *K4, YO, ssk, K1, P1, K1, K2tog, YO, K4, P1; rep from *.

Rnd 6: *K5, YO, ssk, P1, K2tog, YO, K5, P1; rep from *.

Rnd 7: *YO, K3, ssk, K2tog, YO, P1, YO, ssk, K2tog, K3, YO, P1; rep from *.

Rnd 8: *K1, YO, K2, ssk, K2, P1, K2, K2tog, K2, YO, K1, P1; rep from *.

Rnd 9: *K2, YO, K1, ssk, YO, ssk, P1, K2tog, YO, K2tog, K1, YO, K2, P1; rep from *.

Rnd 10: *K3, YO, ssk, K2, P1, K2, K2tog, YO, K3, P1; rep from *.

Rnd 11: *K4, YO, ssk, K1, P1, K1, K2tog, YO, K4, P1; rep from *.

Rnd 12: *K5, YO, ssk, P1, K2tog, YO, K5, P1; rep from *.

Rnd 13: *YO, K3, ssk, K2tog, YO, P1, YO, ssk, K2tog, K3, YO, P1; rep from *.

Rnd 14: *K1, YO, K2, ssk, K2, P1, K2, K2tog, K2, YO, K1, P1; rep from *.

Rnd 15: *K2, YO, K1, ssk, YO, ssk, P1, K2tog, YO, K2tog, K1, YO, K2, P1; rep from *.

Rnd 16: *K3, YO, ssk, K2, P1, K2, K2tog, YO, K3, P1; rep from *.

Rnd 17: *K4, YO, ssk, K1, P1, K1, K2tog, YO, K4, P1; rep from *.

Rnd 18: *K5, YO, ssk, P1, K2tog, YO, K5, P1; rep from *.

Rnd 19: *K5, K2tog, YO, P1, YO, ssk, K5, P1; rep from *.

Rnds 20, 22, 24, and 26: *K7, P1, K7, P1; rep from *.

Rnd 21: *K4, K2tog, YO, K1, P1, K1, YO, ssk, K4, P1; rep from *.

Rnd 23: *K3, K2tog, YO, K2tog, YO, P1, YO, ssk, YO, ssk, K3, P1; rep from *.

Rnd 25: *K2, K2tog, YO, K2tog, YO, K1, P1, K1, YO, ssk, YO, ssk, K2, P1; rep from *.

Rnd 27: *K1, K2tog, YO, K2tog, YO, K2tog, YO, P1, YO, ssk, YO, ssk, YO, ssk, K1, P1; rep from *.

Rnd 28: *K4, P1, K2, P1, K2, P1, K4, P1; rep from *.

Rnd 29: *K2tog, YO, K2tog, YO, P1, YO, ssk, P1, K2tog, YO, P1, YO, ssk, YO, ssk, P1; rep from *.

Rnd 30: *K4, P1, K2, P1, K2, P1, K4, P1; rep from *.

Rep rnds 1–30 for patt.

Please note that you will end up with a YO at beg of needle on rnds 1, 7, and 13. Be careful that the YOs don't slip off and get lost!

Cuff

CO 64 (80) sts loosely. Distribute sts per needle as follows: (16, 32, 16), (32, 16, 32). Join, being careful not to twist sts. Work K3, P1 ribbing for 1½", or desired cuff length.

Leg

Beg mermaid tail lace patt, work rnds 1–30 twice, then rnds 1–18 once more. The leg should measure approximately 7½" from CO.

Heel Flap

K16 (20) sts from needle 1, turn. Sl 1, P31 (39) sts using sts from needles 1 and 3. These 32 (40) sts are heel sts. The rem 32 (40) sts will be on needle 2 for instep sts and are worked later.

Work heel sts as follows.

Row 1: * Sl 1, K1; rep from * to end.

Row 2: Sl 1, purl to end.

Rep rows 1 and 2 total of 15 (17) times, creating 16 (18) slipped sts along each edge of heel flap.

Heel Turn

Row 1: K18 (22), skp, K1, turn.

Row 2: Sl 1, P5, P2tog, P1, turn.

Row 3: Sl 1, knit to within 1 st of gap, skp (1 st on either side of gap), K1, turn.

Row 4: Sl 1, purl to within 1 st of gap, P2tog, P1, turn.

Rep rows 3 and 4, working 1 additional knit or purl st after sl 1 until all sts have been worked. There are 18 (22) sts on heel flap.

Gusset

Knit first half of heel sts onto one needle. Knit second half onto another needle. With second needle, PU 16 (18) sts along RH side of heel. With an empty needle, work across 32 (40) instep sts as follows: K0 (4), work 2 reps of mermaid tail lace patt, end K0 (4).

With rem needle, PU 16 (18) sts along LH side of heel, then work across rem heel sts. You should have half of heel sts plus the right gusset sts on needle 1, instep sts on needle 2, and left gusset sts plus rem heel sts on needle 3. Sts per needle: (20, 32, 20), (34, 40, 34).

Gusset Decrease

Rnd 1

Needle 1: Knit to last 3 sts, K2tog, K1.

Needle 2: Work instep in patt as established in gusset.

Needle 3: K1, ssk, knit to end.

Rnd 2

Needle 1: Knit.

Needle 2: Work instep in established patt.

Needle 3: Knit.

Rep rnds 1 and 2 until 64 (80) sts rem. Sts per needle (16, 32, 16), (20, 40, 20).

Foot

Cont mermaid tail lace patt as established on instep sts (needle 2) and St st on sole sts (needles 1 and 3) until foot measures 1¾ (2)" less than desired length. This lace patt looks best if stopped after working rnds 6, 12, 18, or 30. If you are close to desired foot length and have just completed one of these rnds, you may wish to work your rem length in St st.

Toe Shaping

Rnd 1

Needle 1: Knit to last 3 sts, K2tog, K1.

Needle 2: K1, ssk, knit to last 3 sts, K2tog, K1.

Needle 3: K1, ssk, knit to end.

Rnd 2: Knit.

Rep rnds 1 and 2 until 24 (28) sts rem; 12 (14) heel sts and 12 (14) instep sts. Knit heel sts onto one needle. Graft toe sts tog using Kitchener st (see page 73) or desired grafting method. Weave in ends.

Mermaid Tail Lace Pattern

col	1	2	3	4	5	6	7	8	9	10	11	12	13	14	15	16	Row
	•			•		•			•			•					30
	•	\	○	\	○	•	○	/	•	\	○	•	○	/	○	/	29
	•			•		•			•			•					28
	•		\	○	\	○	\	○	•	○	/	○	/	○	/		27
	•								•								26
	•				\	○	\	○	•	○	/	○	/				25
	•								•								24
	•			\	○	\	○		•		○	/	○	/			23
	•								•								22
	•					\	○		•		○	/					21
	•								•								20
	•						\	○	•	○	/						19
	•						○	/	•	\	○						18
	•					○	/		•		\	○					17
	•				○	/			•			\	○				16
	•			○	/	○	/		•		\	○	\	○			15
	•		○	/					•					\	○		14
	•	○					/	\	○	•	○	/	\			○	13
	•					○	/		•		\	○					12
	•				○	/			•			\	○				11
	•			○	/				•				\	○			10
	•		○	/		○	/		•		\	○		\	○		9
	•	○					/		•		\				○		8
	•	○				/	\	○	•	○	/	\				○	7
	•					○	/		•		\	○					6
	•				○	/			•			\	○				5
	•			○	/				•				\	○			4
	•		○			/			•			\			○		3
	•	○				/			•			\				○	2
	•	○			/	\		○	•	○	/	\				○	1

16-st rep

Key

☐	K
•	P
/	K2tog
\	ssk
○	YO

HAVANA LACE

Designed by Charlene Schurch

♥ **SKILL LEVEL:** Expert ◼◼◼▭ ♥ **SIZES:** Child's Small (Child's Medium, Women's Small, Women's Extra Large) ♥ **FINISHED FOOT CIRCUMFERENCE:** 5 (6⅜, 7¾, 9¼)" ♥ **SIZING METHOD:** Ⓝ

I have been fascinated with heel structures for a long time; this is a variation of the Strong Heel. Instead of increasing for the heel at the intersection of the instep and sole, the increase here is started at the center back of the sock. This provides more area for patterning on the foot for sandals and an intriguing heel structure to be seen as you walk away. This structure reminds me of a seamed silk stocking from the 1940s. Very elegant!

Materials

1 (2, 2, 2) skeins of JaWoll Superwash by Lang (75% wool, 18% nylon, 7% acrylic; 45 g (incl 5 g reinforcing yarn; 208 yds) in color Red 60 [2]

Set of 5 double-pointed needles in size 1 (2.25 mm.) or size required for gauge

2 stitch markers

Tapestry needle

Gauge

9 sts = 1" in St st worked in the rnd

8 sts = 1" in perforated st patt worked in the rnd

Perforated Stitch Pattern

(Chart at right)

(*Multiple of 3 sts*)

Rnd 1: *K1 tbl, YO, K2tog; rep from *.

Rnd 2: Knit.

Rnd 3: *K1 tbl, ssk, YO; rep from *.

Rnd 4: Knit.

Rep rnds 1–4 for patt.

Cuff

CO 42 (54, 66, 78) sts. Distribute sts per needle as follows: (9, 12, 9, 12), (12, 15, 12, 15), (15, 18, 15, 18), (18, 21, 18, 21). Join, being careful not to twist sts. Work in 3-st twisted ribbing as follows:

Rnd 1: *K1 tbl, P2; rep from *.

Rnd 2: *K1, P2; rep from *.

Rep rnds 1 and 2 until ribbing measures 1½".

Leg

Beg perforated st patt and work until leg and cuff measures 3¼ (5, 6¾, 8)" or desired length. End having worked rnd 1 or 3.

Heel

This next rnd is worked on rnd 2 or 4, so it is just knitting around and setting up sts on needles. Knit across needles 1 and 2. K1 from needle 3 and place on needle 2. Complete the rnd, and then rearrange with new st count on needles as follows: (9, 13, 10, 10), (12, 16, 13, 13), (15, 19, 16, 16), (18, 22, 19,

19). Look at the patts at this point: Needle 1 starts with a twisted st, needle 2 starts and ends with a twisted st, needle 3 starts with second st of perforated st patt, needle 4 starts with third st of perforated st patt.

Rnd 1

Needles 1 and 2: Work in established perforated st patt.

Needle 3: Work in established perforated st patt (beg with second st of patt) for 9 (12, 15, 18) sts, pm, YO, K1.

Needle 4: K1, YO, pm, work in established perforated st patt to end.

Rnd 2: Knit.

Rep rnds 1 and 2 until there are 18 (24, 30, 36) sts on each of needle 3 and needle 4.

Sts per needle should be (9, 13, 18, 18), (12, 16, 24, 24), (15, 19, 30, 30), (18, 22, 36, 36).

Heel Turn

Work short rows back and forth on needles 3 and 4.

Row 1 (RS): Knit across first dpn (center of heel); K1, ssk, K1, turn.

Row 2: Sl 1, P3, P2tog, P1, turn. Note that there will be a small gap between working sts that form heel turn and unworked sts.

Row 3: Sl 1, knit to within 1 st of gap, ssk (1 st on either side of gap), K1, turn.

Row 4: Sl 1, purl to within 1 st of gap, P2tog, P1 turn.

Rep rows 3 and 4, working 1 additional knit or purl st after sl 1 until there are 20 (26, 32, 38) sts on needles 3 and 4 for a total of 42 (54, 66, 78) sts.

Foot

Cont established perforated st patt on instep remembering there is 1 additional st at end of needle 2. Cont in established perforated st patt on instep sts and in St st on sole until foot measures 3⅜ (5⅛, 7¼, 8¾)" or desired length. End foot after having worked sts on sole.

Toe Shaping

Needles 1 and 2: Instep sts.

Needles 3 and 4: Sole sts.

Sts per needle (11, 11, 10, 10) (14, 14, 13, 13), (17, 17, 16, 16), (20, 20, 19, 19).

Rnd 1

Needle 1: K1, ssk, knit to end.

Needle 2: Knit to last 3 sts, K2tog, K1.

Needle 3: K1, ssk, knit to end.

Needle 4: Knit to last 3 sts, K2tog, K1.

Rnd 2: Knit.

Rep rnds 1 and 2 until there are 12 (16, 20, 24) total sts. Place sts from instep on one needle and sts from sole onto second needle. Graft toe sts tog using Kitchener st (see page 73) or desired grafting method. Weave in ends.

Perforated Stitch Pattern

			4
o	\	ꝗ	3
			2
/	o	ꝗ	1

3-st rep

Key

☐	K
/	K2tog
\	ssk
o	YO
ꝗ	K1 tbl

DAYDREAMER

Designed by Alyson Johnson

♥ **SKILL LEVEL:** Expert ◼◼◼◻ ♥ **SIZES:** Child's Large (Women's Small, Women's Medium)
♥ **FINISHED FOOT CIRCUMFERENCE:** Approx 6¾ (7½, 8¼)" ♥ **SIZING METHOD:** Ⓝ

Alyson considered both the theme of the sock club and her knowledge of cashmere to use a lace ribbing pattern that helps the sock maintain memory when knit. She designed toe up to ensure that every last bit of the cashmere could be used, but this could easily be converted to top down as the pattern is easy to flip around. This pattern translates well to other sock yarns in a similar weight. Flowers were knit and sewn to the cuff and heel for a touch of whimsy.

CASHMERE AND SIZING

Cashmere is a very fine fiber—that's what makes it so soft. However, because of the fiber's light nature, it can be less resilient than wool, so you may find it will stretch more easily than wool. This is why the design is lacy, but ribbing-based for a snug fit. Because of the fineness of the cashmere fiber, for a perfect fit you may want to knit the socks a little smaller than you normally would. Be extra gentle when you wash cashmere socks!

Materials

I skein in Cashmere Sock Yarn by Zen Yarn Garden; Roxanne Yeun, dyer (100% cashmere; 2 oz; 400 yds) in color First Kiss (2)

Set of 5 double-pointed needles in size 1 (2.25 mm) or size required for gauge

Tapestry needle

Gauge

9 sts = 1" in St st worked in the rnd

Lace Pattern for Foot

(Chart on page 46)

(*Multiple of 6 sts + 4 sts*)

Rnd 1: P1, K2, *P1, K2; rep from * to last st, P1.

Rnd 2: P1, K2, *YO, ssk, P1, K2; rep from * to last st, P1.

Rnd 3: As rnd 1.

Rnd 4: P1, K2, *P1, K2tog, YO, P1, K2; rep from * to last st, P1.

Rep rnds 1–4 for patt.

Lace Pattern for Leg

(Chart on page 46)

(*Multiple of 6 sts*)

Rnd 1: *P1, K2; rep from *.

Rnd 2: *P1, K2, P1, YO, ssk; rep from *.

Rnd 3: As rnd 1.

Rnd 4: *P1, K2, P1, K2tog, YO; rep from *.

Rep rnds 1–4 for patt.

Toe

CO 24 sts using "Becker Toe Cast On" (see page 71). Divide sts evenly on 4 dpns; 6 sts per needle. Needles 1 and 2 will be the first half of rnd (top of foot.) Needles 3 and 4 will be second half of rnd (bottom of foot.)

Inc Rnds

Rnd 1: All needles: Knit.

Rnd 2

Needle 1: K1, K1f&b, knit to end.

Needle 2: Knit to last 2 sts, K1f&b, K1.

Needle 3: K1, K1f&b, knit to end.

Needle 4: Knit to last 2 sts, K1f&b, K1.

Rep rnds 1 and 2 until there are 64 (68, 76) sts total; 16 (17, 19) sts per needle.

Cont to rep rnds 1 and 2 as modified below for your size.

For Small: Inc only on needles 1 and 2 once—66 sts total, (17, 17, 16, 16) per needle.

For Medium: Inc only on needles 3 and 4 twice—72 sts total, (17, 17, 19, 19) per needle.

For Large: Inc only on needles 1 and 2 once—78 sts total, (20, 20, 19, 19) per needle.

Foot

Needles 1 and 2 (instep sts): Work lace patt for foot.

Needles 3 and 4 (sole sts): Knit.

Cont in lace patt until foot measures approx 2½" shorter than desired length, ending with needle 2 of rnd 4 of chart.

Short-Row Heel

See "Wrap and Turn (w&t)" on page 72.

The heel is worked back and forth on 32 (38, 38) sts on needles 3 and 4.

Row 1: Knit 31 (37, 37) sts, w&t last st.

Row 2: Purl to last st, w&t last st.

Row 3: Knit to last unworked st, w&t this st.

Row 4: Purl to last unworked st, w&t this st.

Rep rows 3 and 4 until there are 14 unworked sts in center of heel ending with a purl row.

NARROWER OR WIDER HEEL

For a narrow heel, leave fewer unworked stitches; for a wider heel, leave more unworked stitches.

Cont as follows.

Row 1: Knit unwrapped sts to first wrapped st, knit st and wrap tog, w&t next st (which will now have 2 wraps).

Row 2: Purl to first wrapped st, purl st and wrap tog, w&t the next st (which will now have 2 wraps).

Row 3: Knit to first double-wrapped st, knit *both* wraps and st tog, w&t next st.

Row 4: Purl to first double-wrapped st, purl *both* wraps and st tog, w&t next st.

Rep rows 3 and 4 until all sts have been worked and short-row heel is complete.

Knit across heel sts on needles 3 and 4.

Leg

Work lace patt for leg on all needles. There are 11 (12, 13) reps on each rnd. Work until leg measures 6 (7¼, 8)" from base of heel or desired length, ending with rnd 4.

Cuff

Work cuff in P1, K2 ribbing for 12 rnds (approx 1").

BO sts using a stretchy method (see page 72 for more information if needed). Weave in ends.

Flower Embellishment

(Optional)

Using 2 dpns, CO 35 sts.

K1, BO 5—there are now 2 sts on RH needle; rep K1, BO 5 to end of row—there will be 10 sts on needle.

Break working yarn and thread through a darning needle. Slide sts to other end of dpn; pull needle and yarn through all sts. Pull yarn tight and tie off; do not trim ends. Set flower aside and rep this process for as many flowers desired.

Finishing

Arrange and pin flowers in place on sock with yarn ends at back. Thread darning needle with one yarn end and sew flower in place. Secure second yarn end, then trim both. Sew rem flowers in place— check sewing often to ensure cuff rems stretchy.

Lace Pattern for Foot

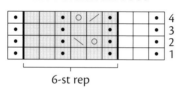

6-st rep

Lace Pattern for Leg

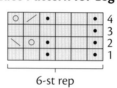

6-st rep

Key

K
P
K2tog
ssk
YO

GLUTTONY

♥ **SKILL LEVEL:** Expert ◼◼◼◻ ♥ **SIZES:** Adult's Small (Large) ♥ **FINISHED FOOT CIRCUMFERENCE:**
7½ (8¾)" ♥ **SIZING METHOD:** Ⓝ ♥ *Note that the designer anticipates 1" of negative ease in this sock*
(sock will fit a foot 1" larger than finished sock).

These socks were designed with a gluttony of color: three softened primary colors were
used and blended to create a gradation effect across each skein of yarn. All four skeins
were dyed so that the colors will gradually transition seemingly magically from one to
the next as the socks are knit.

Materials

1 regular (big foot) set* of 4 Gradiance colors in Verve from Unique Sheep [100% superwash merino wool; 100 (150) g total; 400 (600) yds total] in colorway Glee from the Gradiance collection **1**

Set of 5 double-pointed needles in size 1 (2.25 mm) or size required for gauge

Tapestry needle

A regular set contains 4 skeins, each 25 g; the big foot set contains 4 skeins, each 37.5 g.

ABOUT GRADIANCE YARNS

The Gradiance dyeing technique was invented by Kelly, and is exclusive to The Unique Sheep. She developed a way of dyeing yarn so that as a set of four skeins is used, your project will gradually change from one hand-painted color to the next. Some sets have a dramatic shift in color, and others have more subtle transition. The gradually transitioned sets will work well to show off more complicated stitch patterns and lacework because each skein is "almost" solid.

Gauge

9 sts = 1" in St st worked in the rnd

Slip-Stitch Pattern

(Chart on facing page)

(*Multiple of 6 sts*)

Rnd 1: *P2, K1, P3; rep from *.

Rnds 2, 4, and 6: *K2, sl 1, K3; rep from *.

Rnds 3, 5, and 7: Knit.

Rnd 8: *P5, K1; rep from *.

Rnds 9, 11, and 13: *K5, sl 1; rep from *.

Rnds 10, 12, and 14: Knit.

Rep rnds 1–14.

Cuff

The instructions are written starting at color 1 and ending with color 4. You may reverse this sequence or make one sock each way. Make them both the same or make a fraternal pair.

Color transition happens about halfway down the leg (1), at the heel flap (2), and at the completion of the gusset decrease (3).

Using color 1, CO 76 (88) sts. Divide sts evenly on 4 needles; 19 (22) per needle. Join, being careful not to twist the sts. Work K2, P2 ribbing for 1½".

Leg

Knit 1 rnd and evenly dec 4 sts—72 (84) sts total, 18 (21) on each needle.

Knit 1 rnd.

Work 1 rep of slip-stitch patt.

Rep rnds 1–14 (ending on rnd 13 for Small size), beg color transition indicated below on rnd 12 of patt rep or when you are about halfway down leg. For people using a 150 g set of yarn, if you desire a longer sock leg, rep sl-st patt through rnd 14 once or twice more, ending on rnd 13 of last rep.

Color Transition 1

Change colors as indicated below.

2 rnds color 2

4 rnds color 1

3 rnds color 2

3 rnds color 1

4 rnds color 2

2 rnds color 1

Leg Shaping

Rnd 28: K1, K2tog, knit to last 3 st, ssk, K1—70 (82) sts total; sts per needle (17, 18, 18, 17) (20, 21, 21, 20).

Rnd 29: P1, K1, *P5, K1; rep from *, end P2.

Rnds 30, 32, and 34: K1, sl 1, *K5, sl 1; rep from *, end K2.

Rnds 31 and 33: Knit.

Rnd 35: K1, K2tog, knit to last 3 sts, ssk, K1—68 (80 sts total; sts per needle (16, 18, 18, 16) (19, 21, 21, 19).

Rnd 36: P3,*K1, P5; rep from *, end K1, P4.

Rnds 37, 39, and 41: K3, *sl 1, K5; rep from *, end sl 1, K4.

Rnds 38 and 40: Knit.

Rnd 42: K1, K2tog, knit to last 3 sts, ssk, K1—66 (78) sts; sts per needle (15, 18, 18, 15) (18, 21, 21, 18).

Rnd 43: *P5, K1; rep from *.

Rnds 44, 46, and 48: *K5, sl 1; rep from *.

Rnds 45 and 47: Knit.

Rnd 49: K1, K2tog, knit to last 3 st, ssk, K1—64 (76) sts total; sts per needle (14, 18, 18, 14) (17, 21, 21, 17).

Rnd 50: P1, *K1, P5; rep from *, end K1, P2.

Rnds 51, 53, and 55: K1, *sl 1, K5; rep from *, end sl 1, K2.

Rnds 52, 54, and 56: Knit.

Rnd 57: P4, *K1, P5; rep from * end K1, P4, K1.

Rnds 58, 60☐*, and 62: K4, *sl 1, K5; rep from *, end sl 1, K4, sl 1.

Rnds 59, 61, and 63: Knit.

Rnd 64: P1, *K1, P5; rep from *, end K1, P2.

☐On rnd 60, beg color transition 2:

2 rnds color 3

4 rnds color 2

3 rnds color 3

3 rnds color 2

4 rnds color 3

2 rnds color 2

Sl 2 sts from end of needle 3 to needle 4 so there are 16 (19) sts on needle 4, and sl 1 st from needle 2 to needle 1 so there are 15 (18) sts on needle 1. Sts per needle: (15, 17, 16, 16), (18, 20, 19, 19).

Work across needle 1 as follows: K1, sl 1, K5, sl 1, K1. Turn work so WS is facing and beg heel flap.

Heel Flap

Heel flap is worked in color transition 2.

Purl across needle 1 and needle 4, carrying color 3 on WS to end of needle 4, turn.

Row 1: K1, *K1, sl 1; rep from *, end K2.

Row 2: Purl.

Rep rows 1 and 2, randomly alternating color 2 and color 3, until heel flap measures 2½" or desired length.

Heel Turn

Row 1: K16 (20), ssk, K1, turn.

Row 2: Sl 1, P4, P2tog, P1, turn.

Row 3: Sl 1, knit to within 1 st of gap, ssk (1 st on either side of gap), K1, turn.

Row 4: Sl 1, purl to within 1 st of gap, P2tog, P1, turn.

Rep rows 3 and 4, working 1 additional knit or purl st after sl 1 until all sts have been worked and you are at the end of a RS row with color 2. There are 18 (21) sts for heel flap.

Gusset

Needle 1: With color 2, PU 21 (23) sts along left side, and sl last st to first instep needle.

Needles 2 and 3: K4, *sl 1, K5; rep from *, end sl 1, K4.

Needle 4: PU 21 (23) sts along other side of heel flap, and sl first picked-up st to last instep needle.

Work heel as follows.

Rnd 1

Needle 1: Knit to last 2 sts, K2tog.

Needles 2 and 3: Work in established patt.

Needle 4: Ssk, knit to end.

Rnd 2: Knit.

Rep rnds 1 and 2 until there 67 (79) sts total.

Beg working color transition 3 at end of gusset decrease.

2 rnds color 4
4 rnds color 3
3 rnds color 4
3 rnds color 3
4 rnds color 4
2 rnds color 3

Optional Arch Shaping

Start where your natural arch begins, just past your heel flap.

Rnd 1: Knit.

Rnd 2: Cont any rem gusset decs, but *K1, sl 1; rep from * on rem heel sts.

Rnd 3: Knit.

Rnd 4: Sl the slipped sts from rnd 2 and knit the knit sts.

Rep rnds 3 and 4 until arch shaping is desired length (approx 2").

Foot

Work 14 rnds of sl-st patt on instep as follows, AT THE SAME TIME work St st on sole.

Rnds 1, 3, 5, 8, 10, and 12: Knit.

Rnds 2 and 4: *K5, sl 1; rep from *, end K5.

Rnd 6: P2, *K1, P5; rep from *, end K1, P2.

Rnds 7, 9, and 11: K2, *sl 1, K5; rep from *, end sl 1, K2.

Rnd 13: *P5, K1; rep from * end P5.

Rnd 14: *K5, sl 1; rep from *, end K5.

Rep these 14 rnds until foot is 1½" from desired length.

Toe Shaping

Toe is worked in color 4.

Dec rnd 1: *K2tog, K4; rep from *, end K2tog, K3, K2tog—55 (65) sts.

Knit 4 rnds.

Dec rnd 2: K1 then slip it to RH needle or needle 4, *K3, K2tog; rep from *—44 (52) sts.

Knit 3 rnds.

Dec rnd 3: *K2, K2tog; rep from *—33 (39) sts.

Knit 2 rnds.

Dec rnd 4: *K1, K2tog; rep from *—22 (26) sts.

Knit 1 rnd.

Dec rnd 5: K2tog around—11 (13) sts.

Dec rnd 6: K2tog 5 (6) times, K1.

Cut yarn and thread tail through rem sts. Weave in ends.

Slip-Stitch Pattern

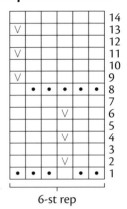

6-st rep

Key

☐	K
•	P
V	sl 1

RAINBOW SWIRL

Designed by Ann McClure

♥ **SKILL LEVEL:** Intermediate ◼◼◼◻ ♥ **SIZES:** Women's Small (Medium, Large)
♥ **FINISHED FOOT CIRCUMFERENCE:** Approx 7 (8, 9)" ♥ **SIZING METHOD:** Ⓝ

A fascinating vortex of stitches streams around the leg and instep of this deceptively complex-looking sock. The simple one-line stitch pattern migrates, thanks to an extra stitch—just be sure to keep your place when the pattern starts to break over the instep.

Materials

1 skein of Celestial Merino Dream* (100% superwash wool, 100 g; 280 m/310 yds) in color Fiesta (2)

Set of 5 double-pointed needles in size 1 (2.25 mm) or size required for gauge

Tapestry needle

This yarn is no longer available. It has been replaced by "Celestial Merino" yarn, which is available in the same colorways, knits to similar gauge, but has 320 m/350 yds per 100 g.

Gauge

7¼ sts = 1" in St st worked in the rnd

Swirl Stitch Pattern

Every rnd: (K2tog, YO, K5) around.

The following information will be useful for working the patt on the instep and fixing any errors. In working the patt on the second and all following rounds, the second st of the K2tog is the K2tog of previous rnd. After making the YO, the next st you work will be the YO of previous rnd. When the 2 sts for the K2tog are divided between two needles, slip the last st on the left-hand needle to the next needle and cont in patt.

Cuff

CO 52 (56, 60) sts. Divide sts evenly on 4 dpns; 13 (14, 15) sts per needle. Join, being careful not to twist sts. Work K2, P2 ribbing for 14 rnds.

Rnd 15: Work in ribbing patt as established and AT THE SAME TIME,

For Small: Dec 1 st at beg of needles 1 and 3 (50 sts).

For Medium: Inc 1 st at beg of needle 1 (57 sts).

For Large: Inc 1 st at beg of each needle (64 sts).

Leg

Rnd 16: Knit even.

Rnd 17: Beg swirl st patt: *K2tog, YO, K5; rep from *. Note that the patt migrates 1 st each rnd, which is why the multiple does not go into the sts evenly.

Rep patt rnd until leg measures 6 (6¾, 7½)" from CO edge or desired length.

Heel Flap

The heel flap is worked back and forth in rows in St st. Because the patt rep has moved around the sock, it is necessary to ensure that sts to be worked for heel flap do not beg or end with a YO. Work next 24 (28, 32) sts on needle 1. Arrange rem 26 (29, 32) sts on needles 3 and 4 for instep as follows: (13, 13), (14, 15), (16, 16). Examine sts on needle 1. If your heel flap beg or ends with a YO, sl first 1 or 2 sts on needle 1 to needle 4 and work 1 or 2 additional sts onto needle 1 to achieve correct number without a YO as first or last st. Set spare needle aside. Work heel flap back and forth in St st for 23 (25, 27) more rows, ending with a WS row.

Heel Turn

Row 1 (RS): Sl 1, K14 (16, 18) ssk, K1, turn.

Row 2: Sl 1, P7, P2tog, P1, turn.

Row 3: Sl 1, knit to within 1 st of gap, ssk (1 st on either side of gap), K1, turn.

Row 4: Sl 1, purl to within 1 st of gap, P2tog, P1, turn.

Rep rows 3 and 4, working 1 additional knit or purl st after sl 1 until all side sts are worked, ending with a WS (purl) row. There are 16 (18, 20) sts on heel flap. Knit across all sts.

Gusset

To resume working instep in patt st as established requires careful attention to detail, since needle 2 will not always beg K2tog, YO. Knit to the st before the K2tog of the previous row and then beg the patt sequence. Also, the last st on needle 3 will sometimes be a YO to maintain the correct number of sts. The sole will be worked in St st.

Work across heel sts with needle 1, PU 13, (14, 15) sts up side of gusset, work instep sts in established patt on needles 2 and 3, with needle 4 PU 13, (14, 15) sts down side of gusset and work 8 (9, 10) heel sts—68 (75, 82) sts total; sts per needle: (21, 13, 13, 21), (23, 14, 15, 23), (25, 16, 16, 25). Beg of rnd is now in center of sole.

Gusset Decrease

Rnd 1

Needle 1: Knit.

Needles 2 and 3: Work instep sts in established patt. Remember that patt migrates 1 st each rnd.

Needle 4: Knit.

Rnd 2 (dec rnd)

Needle 1: Knit to last 3 sts, K2tog, K1.

Needles 2 and 3: Work instep sts in established patt.

Needle 4: K1, ssk, knit to end.

Rep rnds 1 and 2 until 50 (57, 64) sts rem.

Foot

Cont St st on needles 1 and 4, and swirl st patt on needles 2 and 3 until foot measures 7 (7¾, 8¼)" or 1½ (1¾, 2)" less than desired length.

Toe Shaping

Work 1 rnd in St st and dec 2 (1, 0) sts on needles 2 and/or 3 as needed to achieve 12 (14, 16) sts per needle—48 (56, 64) sts total.

Rnd 1

Needle 1: Knit to last 3 sts, K2tog, K1.

Needle 2: K1, ssk, knit to end.

Needle 3: Knit to last 3 sts, K2tog, K1.

Needle 4: K1, ssk, knit to end.

Rnd 2: Knit.

Work rnd 1 followed by rnd 2 worked 3 times.

(Work rnd 1 followed by rnd 2 worked 2 times) twice.

Work rnd 1 followed by rnd 2 worked 1 time.

Work rnds 1 and 2 until 5 sts rem on each needle (20 sts total).

Place instep sts (needles 2 and 3) onto one needle. Knit sts on needle 4 with needle 1.

Graft toe sts tog using Kitchener st (see page 73) or desired grafting method. Weave in ends.

WAVY

Designed by Bindu Gupta

♥ **SKILL LEVEL:** Expert ◗◖◖◖◗ ♥ **SIZES:** Child's Medium (Adult's Medium, Adult's Extra Large)
♥ **FINISHED FOOT CIRCUMFERENCE:** Approx 6 (8, 10)" ♥ **SIZING METHOD:** Ⓝ

This easy lace pattern might make a first lace pattern. It's easy to work and yet looks interesting and more challenging than it actually is. The gentle undulations of the lace create waves, which make the leg look long and elegant.

Materials

2 (2, 3) skeins of Baby Ull from Dale of Norway (100% superwash wool; 50 g; 191 yds/175 m) in color 2908 🄲

Set of 5 double-pointed needles in size 2 (2.75 mm) or size required for gauge

Tapestry needle

Gauge

8 sts = 1" in St st worked in the rnd

Wavy Pattern

(Chart at right)

(*Multiple of 8 sts*)

The written instructions beg with an extra st (indicated in brackets) and the chart beg with a separate column. The extra st has been added to balance the patt on the instep and is worked only once at beg of instep. For leg, work only 8-st patt rep of written instructions or on chart.

Rnds 1, 3, and 5: [K1] *K1, YO, K1, YO, K2tog tbl, K2tog, K2; rep from *.

Rnd 2 and all even-numbered rnds: Knit.

Rnds 7, 9, and 11: [K1] *K1, K2tog tbl, K2tog, YO, K1, YO, K2; rep from *.

Rnd 12: Knit.

Rep rnds 1–12.

Cuff

CO 48 (64, 80) sts. Distribute sts per needle as follows: (8, 16, 8, 16), (16, 16, 16, 16), (16, 24, 16, 24). (Irregular distribution is so that you are working complete reps of wavy patt on each needle). Join, being careful not to twist sts, and work K1, P1 ribbing for 1½".

Leg

Work in wavy patt until leg measures 3¾ (6¾, 7½)" from CO or desired length, ending with even-numbered patt rnd.

Heel Flap

The heel flap is worked back and forth in rows on 23 (31, 39) sts. To set up heel flap, unknit last st of rnd just completed, and place it on needle 1. Sl sts from needle 4 to needle 3 to work heel flap. Set needle 4 aside. Sts per needle: (9, 16, 23), (17, 16, 31), (17, 24, 39). Turn work to beg heel

with WS row on needle 3.

Row 1 (WS): K3, purl to end.

Row 2: P3, *K1, sl 1; rep from * to last 4 sts, K4.

Rep rows 1 and 2 until you have 24 (32, 40) heel flap rows (or desired length for heel), end by working RS row.

Heel Turn

Row 1 (WS): Sl 1, P12 (16, 20) sts, P2tog, P1, turn.

Row 2: Sl 1, K4, ssk, K1, turn.

Row 3: Sl 1, purl to within 1 st of gap, P2tog (1 st on either side of gap), P1, turn.

Row 4: Sl 1, knit to within 1 st of gap, ssk, K1, turn.

Rep rows 3 and 4, working 1 additional knit or purl st after sl 1 until all side sts are worked, end with RS (knit) row. There are 13 (17, 21) sts on heel flap.

For ease of instructions, beg of rnd is now at center bottom of foot. Rearrange and renumber needles as follows: Sl 6 (8, 10) sts from RH side of heel sts to spare needle you set aside to work heel flap. LH side of heel flap sts are on needle 1. Needle 1 is beg of rnd.

Gusset

With needle 1, PU 11 (15, 19) sts from side of heel flap, PU 2 sts at top of gusset (see page 72). With needles 2 and 3 (at this point beg working extra st at beg of instep from chart or written instructions), work wavy patt across instep sts. With needle 4, PU 2 sts at top of gusset, PU 11 (15, 19) sts from side of heel flap, knit rem heel flap sts onto needle 4. Sts per needle: (20, 9, 16, 19), (26, 17, 16, 25), (32, 17, 24, 31). There are an odd number of sts on instep; the extra st will balance patt on instep.

Gusset Decrease

Close Gusset Top

Needle 1: Knit to last 2 sts, ssk.

Needles 2 and 3: Work in established wavy patt.

Needle 4: K2 tog, knit to end.

Rnd 1

Needle 1: Knit to last 3 sts, K2tog, K1.

Needle 2 and 3: Work in established wavy patt.

Needle 4: K1, ssk, knit to end.

Rnd 2

Needle 1: Knit.

Needle 2 and 3: Work in established wavy patt.

Needle 4: Knit.

Rep rnds 1 and 2 until 48 (64, 80) total sts rem. Sts per needle: (12, 9, 16, 11), (16, 17, 16, 15), (20, 17, 24, 19).

Foot

Cont in St st on needles 1 and 4 and in established wavy patt on needles 2 and 3 until foot measures 4 (7⅝, 8⅞)" or desired length, ending with rnd 6 or 12; if you need a few more rnds for sufficient length, work them in St st.

Toe Shaping

Knit sts on needle 1. Beg of rnd now shifts to side of foot. Instep sts are on needles 1 and 2, and sole sts are now on needles 3 and 4.

Rnd 1

Needle 1: K1, ssk knit to end.

Needle 2: Knit to last 3 sts, K2tog, K1.

Needle 3: K1, ssk, knit to end of needle.

Needle 4: Knit to last 3 sts, K2tog, K1.

Rnd 2: Knit.

Rep rnds 1 and 2 until 24 (32, 40) total sts rem.

Rep rnd 1 only until 14 (18, 22) total sts rem. You'll end by working last dec rnd on instep (needle 2). There will be an even number of total sts, but instep and sole will have an odd number of sts.

Place sts from instep on one needle and sts from sole onto second needle. Graft toe sts tog using Kitchener st (see page 73) or desired grafting method. Weave in ends.

Wavy Pattern

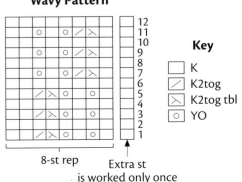

8-st rep

Extra st is worked only once at beg of instep.

Key

☐	K
╱	K2tog
⤬	K2tog tbl
○	YO

RAINBOW OVER LAHAINA

Designed by Adrienne Fong

♥ **SKILL LEVEL:** Expert ◼◼◼◻ ♥ **SIZES:** Women's Small (Medium, Large)
♥ **FINISHED FOOT CIRCUMFERENCE:** Approx 7 (8, 9)" ♥ **SIZING METHOD:** Ⓝ

The lovely wharf town of Lahaina on the island of Maui was the inspiration for this sock. Adrienne loved the gentle rainbows formed by the striping of the yarn, which reminded her of the beautiful skies seen in Hawaii. These make a splendid sandal sock and the thoughts of tropical warmth will keep you cozy all winter long.

Materials

I skein of Meilenweit by Lana Grossa (45% cotton, 42% virgin wool, 13% polyamide; 100 g; 380 m) in color 6503

Set of 5 double-pointed needles in size 1 (2.25 mm) or size required for gauge

Tapestry needle

Gauge

8½ sts = 1" in St st worked in the rnd

Sock sizes can be adjusted by working with a smaller or larger needle to obtain a different gauge.

Rainbow Lace Pattern

(Chart at right)

(*Multiple of 9 sts*)

Rnd 1: *K1, YO, K2, ssk, K2tog, K2, YO; rep from *.

Rnd 2: Knit.

Rnd 3: *YO, K2, ssk, K2tog, K2, YO, K1; rep from *.

Rnd 4: Knit.

Rep rnds 1–4.

Cuff

CO 63 (72, 81) sts. Distribute sts onto 4 dpns (9, 18, 18, 18) (18, 18, 18, 18) (18, 18, 18, 27). Join, being careful not to twist your sts, pm to indicate beg of rnd. (Knit 1 rnd, purl 1 rnd) twice; knit 1 rnd; then beg patt.

Leg

Work in rainbow lace patt until leg and cuff measure 6½ (7, 8)" or desired length, ending on rnd 1 or 3.

Heel Flap

Set up for heel flap: On needle 1, K2 (0, 2), transfer sts just knit to needle 4. K32 (36, 41) rem sts from needle 1 and 2 for heel sts. K31

(36, 40) sts on needles 3 and 4 for instep. There should be 2 sts on either side of complete rainbow lace patt reps for Small and Large sizes. The Medium size contains 36 sts and complete patt reps.

The heel flap is worked back and forth over 32 (36, 41) sts. Place rem 31 (36, 40) sts on a holder for instep.

Eye of Partridge with Garter Ridge Heel Flap

Row 1: Sl 1, K2, purl to last 3 sts, K2, P1.

Row 2: Sl 1, K2, *K1, sl 1; rep from * to last 5 (5, 4) sts, K5 (5, 4).

Row 3: Sl 1, K2, purl to last 3 sts, K2, P1.

Row 4: Sl 1, K4, *sl 1, K1; rep from * to last 3 (3, 4) sts, K3 (3, 4).

Rep rows 1–4 until heel flap measures 2½" or desired length, ending on row 2 or 4.

Heel Turn

Row 1: Sl 1, P18 (20, 23) P2tog, P1, turn.

Row 2: Sl 1, K7 (7, 8) ssk, K1, turn.

Row 3: Sl 1, purl to within 1 st of gap, P2tog (1 st on either side of gap), P1, turn.

Row 4: Sl 1, knit to within 1 st of gap, ssk, K1, turn.

Rep rows 3 and 4, working 1 additional knit or purl st after sl 1 until all sts have been worked. End with a knit row. There are 20 (22, 25) sts on heel flap. Do not turn work.

Gusset

Needle 1: PU 1 st in each slipped st along side of heel.

Needles 2 and 3: K2 (0, 2), work 27 (36, 36) instep sts in established rainbow lace patt, K2 (0, 2).

Needle 4: PU same number of sts along rem side of heel, K10 (11, 12) sts. Beg of rnd is now middle of heel flap.

Gusset Decrease

Rnd 1 (dec rnd)

Needle 1: Knit to last 3 sts, K2tog, K1.

Needles 2 and 3: Work instep in established rainbow lace patt.

Needle 4: K1, ssk, knit to end.

Rnd 2: Knit around as established in rainbow lace patt on instep and in St st on sole.

Rep rnds 1 and 2 until 59 (68, 77) total sts rem; 31 (36, 40) instep sts and 28 (32, 37) sole sts.

Foot

Cont in established rainbow lace patt on instep and St st on sole until foot measures 1¾ (2, 2¼)" less than desired length. End on rnd 2 or 4.

Toe Shaping

Set-up for toe: Dec 3 (4, 4) sts by skipping 1 of the YOs in each patt rep across instep sts only—28 (32, 37) instep sts and 28 (32, 37) sole sts.

Knit sts on needle 1. New beg of rnd is at side of foot.

Rnd 1 (dec rnd)

Needle 1: K1, ssk, knit to end.

Needle 2: Knit to last 3 sts sts, K2tog, K1.

Needle 3: K1, ssk, knit to end.

Needle 4: Knit to last 3 sts, K2tog, K1.

Rnd 2: Knit.

Rep rnds 1 and 2 until 28 (32, 37) total sts rem. Then work rnd 1 (dec rnd) only until 20 (20, 22) total sts rem. Graft toe sts tog using Kitchener st (see page 73) or desired grafting method. Weave in ends.

Rainbow Lace Pattern

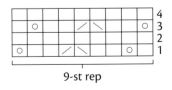

9-st rep

Key

☐	K
╱	K2tog
╲	ssk
○	YO

REIMS

Designed by Alyson Johnson

♥ **SKILL LEVEL:** Expert ◼◼◼◻ ♥ **SIZES:** Women's Small (Large, Extra Large)
♥ **FINISHED FOOT CIRCUMFERENCE:** Approx 7¼ (8½, 9¾)" ♥ **SIZING METHOD:** Ⓝ

These socks were designed for the ART WALK Sock Yarn Club, and Zen Yarn Garden selected Monet as their colorway inspiration. Alyson chose a pattern called Gazebo Lace for this sock. The pattern reminded her of the flying buttresses and architectural elements of the great cathedrals of Europe, especially Reims in France. Her bobble cast on is reminiscent of the peaks and spires of Reims and the heel flap evokes the tall doorways. The pattern looks good in both semisolid and variegated colorways.

Materials

1 skein of Squooshy Yarn from Zen Yarn Garden (80% superwash merino, 20% nylon; 115 g/4 oz; 420 yds) in color Velvet Rose (2)

Set of 5 double-pointed needles in size 1 (2.25 mm) or size required for gauge

Tapestry needle

Gauge

7½ sts = 1" in St st worked in the rnd

Lace Pattern

(Chart at right)

(*Multiple of 10 sts*)

sK2p: Sl 1 st kw, K2tog, pass slipped st over.

Rnd 1: *YO, K3, sK2p, K3, YO, K1; rep from *.

Rnd 2: Knit.

Rnd 3: *K1, YO, K2, sK2p, K2, YO, K1, P1; rep from *.

Rnd 4: *K9, P1; rep from *.

Rnd 5: * K2, YO, K1, sK2p, K1, YO, K2, P1; rep from *.

Rnd 6: As rnd 4.

Rnd 7: *K3, YO, sK2p, YO, K3, P1; rep from *.

Rnd 8: Knit.

Rep rnds 1–8 for patt.

Leg

MB (make bobble): K1, P1, K1 into one st; turn and P1, K1, P1; turn and K1, P1, K1, pass second and third st over first st.

CO 60 (70, 80) sts. Distribute sts per needle as follows: (20, 10, 20, 10), (20, 20, 20, 10), (20, 20, 20, 20). Join, being careful not to twist sts.

First rnd: *K5, MB, K4; rep from *.

Beg lace patt and work until leg measures approx 7½", or desired length, ending with rnd 8. Do not work needle 4 on last rnd 8.

Heel Flap

Combine sts on needles 1 and 4 onto needle 1 for heel flap. Sts per needle: (30, 20, 10) (30, 20, 20) (40, 20, 20).

Work heel flap back and forth.

Row 1: Sl 1, K2, YO, sK2p, YO, K4, *K3, YO, sK2p, YO, K4; rep from * to end.

Row 2: Sl 1, purl to end.

Rep rows 1 and 2 a total of 15 (15, 20) times.

Heel Turn

Row 1: Sl 1, K16 (16, 21), K2tog, K1, turn.

Row 2: Sl 1, P5, P2tog, P1, turn.

Row 3: Sl 1, knit to within 1 st of gap, K2tog (st on either side of gap), K1, turn.

Row 4: Sl 1, purl to within 1 st of gap, P2tog, K1, turn.

Rep row 3 and 4, working 1 additional knit or purl st after sl 1 until all sts have been worked. There are 18 (18, 22) sts on heel flap.

Gusset

Needle 1: Knit across heel sts, PU 16 (16, 21) sts from side of heel flap.

Needles 2 and 3: Work lace patt across instep beg with rnd 1.

Needle 4: PU 16 (16, 21) sts from side of heel flap, K9 (9, 11) from heel flap onto needle 4.

Sts per needle: (25, 20, 10, 25), (25, 20, 20, 25), (32, 20, 20, 32).

Gusset Decrease

Rnd 1

Needle 1: Knit to last 3 sts K2tog, K1.

Needles 2 and 3: Work in established lace patt.

Needle 4: K1, ssk, knit to end.

Rnds 2 and 3

Needle 1: Knit.

Needles 2 and 3: Work in established lace patt.

Needle 4: Knit.

Rep rnds 1–3 until 60 (70, 80) total sts rem; sts per needle: (15, 20, 10, 15), (15, 20, 20, 15), (20, 20, 20, 20).

Foot

Cont rnds 2 and 3 of gusset until foot measures 1½" to 2" less than desired length, ending with rnd 8 of lace patt. If necessary work for desired length in St st.

Toe Shaping

Rearrange sts on needles as follows: (15, 15, 15, 15), (17, 18, 17, 18), (20, 20, 20, 20).

Rnd 1

Needle 1: Knit to last 3 sts, K2tog, K1.

Needle 2: K1, ssk, knit to end.

Needle 3: Knit to last 3 sts, K2tog, K1.

Needle 4: K1, ssk, knit to end.

Rnd 2: Knit.

Rep rnds 1 and 2 until 20 (22, 20) total sts rem.

Knit the sts from needle 1 onto needle 4 and combine sts from needle 2 and 3 onto one needle. Graft toe sts tog using Kitchener st (see page 73) or desired grafting method. Weave in ends.

Lace Pattern

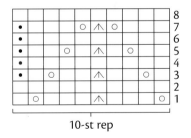

10-st rep

Key

☐ K   ⊙ YO

▣ P   ⃟ sK2p

ROCKS AND TRAILS

Designed by Judy Alexander

♥ **SKILL LEVEL:** Expert ◼◼◼◻ ♥ **SIZES:** Adult's Small (Extra Large)
♥ **FINISHED FOOT CIRCUMFERENCE:** Approx 7⅝ (9¼)" ♥ **SIZING METHOD:** Ⓝ

Judy was inspired to make these socks while hiking in the Colorado mountains near her home. The combination of textured patterning and simple stripes on the foot make these sport-weight-yarn socks great to wear with boots. While made for the outdoors, they're pretty enough to be worn anywhere.

Materials

Bollicine Dolly from Cascade Yarns (100% extrafine shrink-resistant merino wool; 50 g; 153 yds) **2**

A 1 skein in color 01 White

B 1 skein in color M4 Medium Gray

Set of 5 double-pointed needles size 2 (2.75 mm) or size required for gauge

Tapestry needle

Gauge

6½ sts = 1" in rocks and trails patt worked in the rnd

Stitch Pattern Notes

◊ Make sure to strand the yarn loosely when slipping sts, so that your sock has some elasticity. If patt is worked too tightly, the sock will be difficult to put on.

◊ Carry colors down side of sock and along sole, bringing up new color underneath working color. This avoids holes where stripe color changes.

◊ Sl all sts purlwise wyib.

Rocks and Trails Pattern

(Chart at right)

(Multiple of 10 sts)

Rnds 1, 2, 5, and 6: With A, knit.

Rnd 3: With B, * sl 2, K1, sl 2, K5; rep from *.

Rnd 4: With B, *sl 2, P1, sl 2, P5; rep from *.

Rnd 7: With B, * K5 , sl 2, K1, sl 2; rep from *.

Rnd 8: With B, * P5, sl 2, P1, sl 2; rep from *.

Rep rnds 1–4.

Stripe Pattern

Rnds 1 and 2: With B, knit.

Rnds 3 and 4: With A, knit.

Rep rnds 1–4.

Cuff

With A, CO 48 (60) sts. Divide sts evenly on 4 needles; 12 (15) sts per needle. Join, being careful not to twist sts. Work K2, P2 ribbing for 1½". On Small only, inc 2 sts evenly in last row of ribbing—50 sts.

Leg

Beg rocks and trails patt and work until leg, including cuff, measures 6 (7)" or desired leg length. End with rnd 2 or 6. Cut A and work with B only.

Heel Flap

This sock has a Dutch heel.

Heel flap is worked back and forth over 25 (31) sts. Arrange sts as follows: (25, 12, 11), (30, 15, 15).

For Extra Large, inc 1 st in middle of first row of heel flap (31 sts).

Row 1: K3, purl across to last 3 sts, K3.

Row 2: K3, (K1, sl 1) to last 4 sts, K4.

Rep row 1 and 2 until heel flap measures approx 2¼", ending with row 1.

Heel Turn

Row 1: K17 (21), ssk, turn.

Row 2: Sl 1, P9 (11) P2tog, turn.

Row 3: Sl 1, K9 (11), ssk, turn.

Rep rows 2 and 3 until all of the sts have been used. End with row 2.

Gusset

With B, K5 (6) sts from end of heel turn. Beg of rnd is now in center of heel/sole. With new needle 1, K4 (5), K2tog, PU 1 st at edge of each garter ridge along heel flap, plus 1 extra st where instep and heel flap meet. Work across instep on needles 2 and 3, starting with stripe patt row 1. With needle 4, PU 1 st where instep and heel flap meet, and 1 st at edge of each garter ridge along other side of heel flap (the same number of sts as on other side), K5 (6) sts.

Needles 1 and 4 should have same number of sts; these are for sole. Cont in stripe pattern, knit 1 row.

Gusset Decrease

Cont established stripe patt.

Rnd 1

Needle 1: Knit to last 2 sts, K2tog.

Needles 2 and 3: Work in established stripe patt.

Needle 4: Ssk, knit to end.

Rnds 2 and 3: Knit.

Rep rnds 1–3 until there are 49 (60) sts total.

For Small only, dec 1 st on instep sts of next row, so that there are an even number of sts. Sts per needle: (12, 12, 12, 12), (15, 15, 15, 15).

Foot

Cont established stripe patt until foot measures 7½ (8¾)" or desired length (approx 2¼" before total length).

Toe Shaping

Cont established stripe patt while working decs until 8 sts rem on each needle and an A stripe has been completed. Cut A and finish toe in B.

Dec rnd

Needle 1: Knit to last 3 sts, K2tog, K1.

Needle 2: K1, ssk, knit to end.

Needle 3: Knit to last 3 sts. K2tog, K1.

Needle 4: K1, ssk, knit to end.

Work 3 rnds even.

(Work dec rnd, work 2 rnds even) twice.

(Work dec rnd, work 1 rnd even) 3 times.

Work dec rnd every rnd until 8 sts rem on each needle.

Combine sts from needles 1 and 2 onto one needle, and sts from needles 3 and 4 on second needle. The sts from RH side of sock are on one side and sts from LH side are on another needle. When grafted, it gives a mitten-top look to finish of toe. Graft toe sts tog using Kitchener st (see page 73) or desired grafting method. Weave in ends.

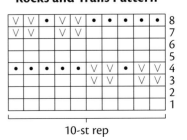

Rocks and Trails Pattern

10-st rep

Key

☐ K   ◦ P   ∨ sl 1

COZY CABLES

Designed by Terry Liann Morris, aka SailingKnitter

♥ **SKILL LEVEL:** Expert ◼◼◼◻ ♥ **SIZES:** Women's Extra Large
♥ **FINISHED FOOT CIRCUMFERENCE:** Approx 9¾" ♥ **SIZING METHOD:** Ⓖ

Ribbing and cables combine to make a comfy sock that is easy to knit and overcomes the tendency of cables to create inelastic fabric. The medallion cable on the leg transitions to a simple rope cable on the top of the foot for greater comfort in shoes. Use a solid or semisolid yarn to show off your cable work.

Materials

2 skeins of Stroll from Knit Picks (75% superwash wool, 25% nylon; 50 g; 231 yds) in color Grass

Set of 4 double-pointed needles in size 1 (2.25 mm) or size required for gauge

Cable needle

Tapestry needle

Gauge

8 sts = 1" in St st worked in the rnd

SIZING OPTIONS

Changing the size of this sock by adding or removing repeats is not possible due to the very large pattern repeat. To moderately increase or decrease the sock size, try increasing or decreasing the needle size to obtain a moderately different stitch gauge. For size changes greater than one full shoe size, go to a heavier- or lighter-weight yarn and matching needles; this will result in a more significant change of gauge. Be sure to swatch to ensure that the size you achieve is the size that you want.

Special Abbreviations

2/2CB: Sl 2 sts to cn and hold at back, K2, K2 from cn.

1/2CBP: Sl 1 st to cn and hold at back, K2, P1 from cn.

2/1CFP: Sl 2 sts to cn and hold at front, P1, K2 from cn.

Ribbing Pattern

(Chart on page 62)

(*Multiple of 14 sts*)

Rnds 1 and 2: *P1, (K2, P2) twice, K4, P1; rep from *.

Rnd 3: *P1, (K2, P2) twice, C4B, P1; rep from *.

Rnd 4: *P1, (K2, P2) twice, K4, P1; rep from *.

Rep rnds 1–4 for patt.

Leg Pattern

(Chart on page 62)

(*Multiple of 14 sts*)

Rnd 1: *P1, 2/1CFP, 1/2CBP, P2, K4, P1; rep from *.

Rnds 2, 4, 5, 6, and 8: * P2, K4, P3, K4, P1; rep from *.

Rnds 3 and 7: *P2, C4B, P3, C4B, P1; rep from *.

Rnd 9: *P1, 1/2CBP, 2/1CFP, P2, K4, P1; rep from *.

Rnd 10: *P1, K6, P2, K4, P1; rep from *.

Rnd 11: *1/2CBP, P2, 2/1CFP, P1, C4B, P1; rep from *.

Rnds 12, 14, 16, and 18: *K8, P1, K4, P1; rep from *.

Rnds 13 and 17: *K2, P4, K2, P1, K4, P1; rep from *.

Rnd 15: *K2, P4, K2, P1, C4B, P1; rep from *.

Rnd 19: *2/1CFP, P2, 1/2CBP, P1, C4B, P1; rep from *.

Rnd 20: *P1, K6, P2, K4, P1; rep from *.

Rep rnds 1–20 for patt.

Instep Pattern

(chart on page 62)

(*Worked over 36 sts*)

Rnd 1: (P2, C4B, P2, K2, P2, K2) 2 times, P2, C4B, P2.

Rnds 2, 3, and 4: (P2, K4, P2, K2, P2, K2) 2 times, P2, K4, P2.

Rep rnds 1–4 for patt.

Cuff

Using twisted German CO (see page 70), CO 84 sts. Divide sts evenly on 3 needles; 28 sts per needle. Join, being careful not to twist sts. Work rnds 1–4 of ribbing patt a total of 4 times.

Leg

Work rnds 1–20 of leg patt a total of 3 times; then work rnds 1–9 once more. Work rnd 1 of ribbing patt once.

Heel Flap

Beg with needle 1, K14 sts, sl rem 14 sts from this needle to needle 2 without working. Turn work. Sl first st as if to purl, purl to end of needle. Without turning, purl 20 sts from needle 3. Sl rem 8 sts to needle 2. You should now have 34 sts on one needle. This is your heel flap and will be worked back and forth. Ignore the 50 sts on the other needle for now.

Row 1: (Sl 1, K1) to end of row.

Row 2: Sl 1, purl to end.

Rep rows 1 and 2 until heel flap is 2½" long, ending after working a purl row.

Heel Turn

Row 1: K19, ssk, K1, turn.

Row 2: Sl 1, P5, P2tog, P1, turn.

Row 3: Sl 1, knit to within 1 st of gap, ssk (1 st on either side of gap), K1, turn.

Row 4: Sl 1, purl to within 1 st of gap, P2tog, P1, turn.

Rep rows 3 and 4, working 1 additional knit or purl st after sl 1 until all side sts are worked—20 heel sts.

Knit all heel sts.

Gusset

Needle 1: With RS facing you, PU 17 sts along one edge of heel flap. K7 from needle 2.

Needle 2: Work 36 sts in instep patt (follow text or chart on page 62).

Needle 3: K7 from needle 2, PU 17 sts along rem heel flap edge. Cont with this same needle, K10 from needle 1.

You are now at center of bottom of heel. This will be the beg/end of all future rnds. You should have 34 sts on needle 1, 36 instep sts on needle 2, and 34 sts on needle 3.

Gusset Decrease

Cont patt rnds for instep sts while working gusset decs as follows.

Rnds 1 and 3

Needle 1: Knit to last 3 sts, K2tog, K1.

Needle 2: Work in established patt.

Needle 3: K1, ssk, knit to end.

Rnds 2 and 4

Needle 1: Knit.

Needle 2: Work in established patt.

Needle 3: Knit.

Rep rnds 1–4 until 21 sts rem on needles 1 and 3—total of 78 sts.

Foot

Cont St st on needles 1 and 3, and established patt on needle 2 until foot measures 8¼" or 2" less than desired length.

Toe Shaping

Dec Rnd:

Needle 1: Knit to last 3 sts, K2tog, K1.

Needle 2: K1, ssk, knit to last 3 sts, K2tog, K1.

Needle 3: K1, ssk, knit to end—74 sts.

Rnds 2 and 3: Knit.

Rnd 4: Work dec rnd—70 sts.

Rnds 5 and 6: Knit.

Rnd 7: Work dec rnd—66 sts.

Rnd 8: Knit.

Rnd 9: Work dec rnd—62 sts.

Rnd 10: Knit.

Rnd 11: Work dec rnd—58 sts.

Rnd 12: Knit.

Rnd 13: Work dec rnd—54 sts.

Rnd 14:

Needle 1: Knit to last 3 sts K2tog, K1.

Needle 2: Knit.

Needle 3: K1, ssk, knit to end—52 sts.

Rnd 15: Work dec rnd—48 sts.

Rnd 16: As rnd 14—46 sts.

Rnd 17: Work dec rnd—42 sts.

Rnd 18: As rnd 14—40 sts.

Rnd 19: Work a dec rnd—36 sts.

Cont working only dec rds until you have 16 sts total rem (4 on first needle, 8 on instep, and 4 on last needle). Graft toe sts tog using Kitchener st (see page 73) or desired grafting method. Weave in ends.

Ribbing Pattern

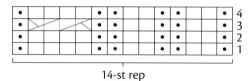

14-st rep

Leg Pattern

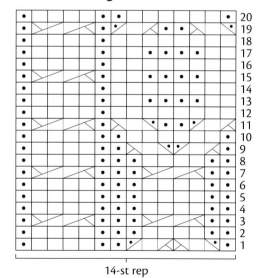

14-st rep

Key

☐ K

• P

▱ 2/2CB: sl 2 sts to cn and hold at back, K2, K2 from cn

▱ 2/1CFP: sl 2 sts to cn and hold at front, P1, K2 from cn

▱ 1/2CBP: sl 1 st to cn and hold at back, K2, P1 from cn

Instep Pattern

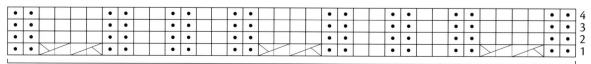

36 sts

♥ **SKILL LEVEL:** Expert ■■■□ ♥ **SIZES:** Women's Medium
♥ **FINISHED FOOT CIRCUMFERENCE:** Approx 8" ♥ **SIZING METHOD:** Ⓖ

The Greed colorway is a mix of muted shades of gold and green, reminiscent of dusty gold and weathered bills. Deb Kessler, the dyer, imagined it as the faded, aging, long-hoarded stash of a miser, while Anne saw the golden color of oak leaves and dried acorns and thought a sock with an autumn theme would work well. This sock was designed to reflect the concept of greed, as inspired by the activity of the (somewhat nefarious) squirrels rushing and competing in Anne's yard to get acorns stashed for winter. The pattern packs plenty of acorn goodness into an ultimately lacy and very wearable fall accessory.

Materials

1 skein of Superwash Merino Wool Sock Yarn from Fearless Fibers (100% superwash merino; 4 oz; 550 yds) in color Greed

Set of 4 double-pointed needles in size 1 (2.25 mm), or size required for gauge

Tapestry needle

Gauge

8 sts = 1" in St st worked in the rnd

Acorn Lace Pattern

(Chart on facing page)

Written instructions below are for leg only; work patt rep below (or on chart) 3 times.

For instep, work across all sts on chart once.

Inc to 7 sts: Knit into front, back, front, back, front, back, front of next st to make 7 sts out of 1 st.

CCD: Sl 2 sts kw tog, K1, pass 2 slipped sts over st just knit.

Rnd 1: *K1, P1, K11, P1, K1, P1, K5, P1; rep from *.

Rnd 2: *K1, P1, ssk, YO, ssk, K3, K2tog, YO, K2tog, P1, K1, P1, ssk, YO, inc to 7 sts, YO, K2tog, P1; rep from *.

Rnd 3: *K1, P1, K9, P1, K1, P1, K2, P7, K2, P1; rep from *.

Rnd 4: *K1, P1, ssk, YO, ssk, K1, K2tog, YO, K2tog, P1, K1, P1, ssk, YO, P7, YO, K2tog, P1; rep from *.

Rnd 5: *K1, P1, K7, P1, K1, P1, K2, P7, K2, P1; rep from *.

Rnd 6: *K1, P1, ssk, YO, CCD, YO, K2tog, P1, K1, P1, ssk, YO, P7, YO, K2tog, P1; rep from *.

Rnd 7: *K1, P1, K5, P1, K1, P1, K11, P1; rep from *.

Rnd 8: *K1, P1, ssk, YO, inc to 7 sts, YO, K2tog, P1, K1, P1, ssk, YO, ssk, K3, K2tog, YO, K2tog, P1; rep from *.

Rnd 9: *K1, P1, K2, P7, K2, P1, K1, P1, K9, P1; rep from *.

Rnd 10: *K1, P1, ssk, YO, P7, YO, K2tog, P1, K1, P1, ssk, YO, ssk, K1, K2tog, YO, K2tog, P1; rep from *.

Rnd 11: *K1, P1, K2, P7, K2, P1, K1, P1, K7, P1; rep from *.

Rnd 12: *K1, P1, ssk, YO, P7, YO, K2tog, P1, K1, P1, ssk, YO, CCD, YO, K2tog, P1; rep from *.

Rep rnds 1–12.

Cuff

CO 66 sts. Divide sts evenly on 3 needles; 22 sts per needle. Join, being careful not to twist sts. Work K1, P1 ribbing until cuff measures 1½".

Leg

Work acorn lace patt rep for leg 3 times, and work rnds 1–12 a total of 5 times or to desired length to start of heel (change length by adding or subtracting full patt reps). End last rep on rnd 11.

Rnd 12: Work first 31 sts of rnd in patt and place on needle 1. Then, MIP, work rem sts of rnd in patt, and end with MIP after last st. Divide 37 instep sts just worked over needles 2 and 3.

Heel Flap

With RS facing you, work heel flap back and forth on needle 1.

Row 1 (RS): Knit.

Row 2: (Sl 1, P1) 5 times, P11, (P1, sl 1) 5 times.

Row 3: K12, YO, ssk, K3, K2tog, YO, K12.

Row 4: (Sl 1, P1) 6 times, P7, (P1, Sl 1) 6 times.

Row 5: K13, YO, ssk, K1, K2tog, YO, K13.

Row 6: (Sl 1, P1) 7 times, P3, (P1, sl 1) 7 times.

Row 7: K14, YO, CCD, YO, K14.

Row 8: (Sl 1, P1) 7 times, P3, (P1, sl 1) 7 times.

Row 9: Knit.

Row 10: *Sl 1, P1; rep from * to last st, sl 1.

Rep rows 9 and 10 eleven times more, then work row 9 once more (33 total heel flap rows).

Heel Turn

Row 1 (WS): Sl 1, P17, P2tog, P1, turn.

Row 2 (RS): Sl 1, K6, ssk, K1, turn.

Row 3: Sl 1, purl to within 1 st of gap, P2tog (1 st on either side of gap), P1, turn.

Row 4: Sl 1, knit to within 1 st of gap, ssk, K1, turn.

Rep rows 3 and 4, working 1 additional knit or purl st after sl 1 until all heel sts have been worked, ending last purl row with P1, and last knit row with K1. There are 19 heel sts.

Divide the heel sts onto 2 needles with 10 sts on needle with yarn attached (needle 1) and 9 sts on a spare needle. Place 37 instep sts currently on needles 2 and 3 onto one needle, which will become needle 2.

Gusset

With RS facing, and needle 1, PU 17 sts along heel flap, through large slipped sts at edge. Using a spare dpn, work row 1 of acorn lace patt across 37 instep sts on needle 2. Using empty dpn (now needle 3), PU 17 sts along other heel flap and knit across rem 9 heel sts from spare needle. From this point, rnds beg and end at center of heel.

Gusset Decrease

Rnd 1

Needle 1: Knit to last st, P1.

Needle 2: Work established acorn lace patt on instep.

Needle 3: P1, knit to end.

Rnd 2

Needle 1: Knit to the last 3 sts, K2tog, P1.

Needle 2: Work established acorn lace patt on instep.

Needle 3: P1, ssk, knit to end.

Rep rnds 1 and 2 until there are 17 sts on needle 1 and 16 sts on needle 3.

Foot

Work even as follows.

Needle 1: Knit to last st, P1.

Needle 2: Work established acorn lace patt on instep.

Needle 3: P1, knit to end.

Cont until foot measures desired length to beg of toes minus approx ½", end on row 6 or 7.

Next rnd:

Needle 1: Knit.

Needle 2: Knit across and inc 2 sts evenly spaced.

Needle 3: Knit—total 66 sts.

Work 6 rnds in knit, or enough to achieve desired foot length to beg of toes.

Toe Shaping

Rnd 1

Needle 1: Knit to last 3 sts, K2tog, K1.

Needle 2: K1, ssk, knit across to last 3 sts, K2tog, K1.

Needle 3: K1, ssk, knit to end.

Rnd 2: Knit around.

Rep rnds 1 and 2 until 26 total sts rem; 7 sts on needle 1, 13 sts on needle 2, and 6 sts on needle 3. Knit across needle 1 and place those sts on needle 3 so that sts are now on 2 needles. Graft toe sts tog using Kitchener st (see page 73) or desired grafting method. Weave in ends.

Acorn Lace Pattern

Work 22-st rep for leg 3 times.
(St count varies from rnd to rnd and returns to original number of sts on rnds 1, 6, 7, and 12.)

Work 37-st instep patt only once across all sts on needle 2.
(St count varies from rnd to rnd and returns to original number of sts on rnds 1 and 12.)

Key

☐	K	○	YO
•	P	⋊	CCD: sl 2 kw tog, K1, p2sso
╱	K2tog	⩔	Inc to 7 sts
╲	ssk	▨	No st

TEATIME

Designed by Adrienne Fong

♥ **SKILL LEVEL:** Expert ■■■□ ♥ **SIZES:** Adult Small (Large)
♥ **FINISHED FOOT CIRCUMFERENCE:** Approx 7½ (8½)" ♥ **SIZING METHOD:** **G** **M**

Slipped-stitch or mosaic patterns look complicated but are actually very easy because only one color of yarn is used per round. So, get your favorite teacup and make yourself a pot of your favorite tea. Enjoy Teatime—and don't forget the biscuits!

Materials

Meilenweit from Lana Grossa (80% virgin wool, 20% nylon; 50g; 230 yds/210 m) **2**

A 1 skein of color 1335 (darker)

B 1 skein of color 1334 (lighter)

Set of 5 double-pointed needles in size 1½ (2.5 mm) and size 2 (2.75 mm) or size required for gauge

2 stitch markers

Tapestry needle

Gauge

8½ sts = 1" in St st worked in the rnd on smaller needles

8½ sts = 1" in mosaic patt worked in the rnd on larger needles

Mosaic Pattern for Sole

Work over 19 (23) sole sts as indicated in "Gusset Decrease" above right.

Rnds 1 and 2: With B, (sl 1, K2) 3 times, (sl 1, K1) 0 (2) times, (sl 1, K2) 3 times, K1.

Rnds 3 and 4: With A, knit.

Rep rnds 1–4 for patt.

Cuff

Two-color cuff: Using smaller needles and A, CO 64 (72) sts. Divide sts evenly on 4 needles; 16 (18) sts per needle. Join, being careful not to twist sts. Cut A, leaving end long enough to weave in. With B, knit 1 rnd. Work K2, P2 ribbing until cuff measures 1½".

Optional plain cuff: CO with B and work entire cuff with B.

Leg

(Mosaic chart on page 68)

Using larger needles and A, knit 1 rnd inc 0 (4) sts evenly around—64 (76) sts.

Knit 1 rnd. Do not cut A. With B, for both sizes beg mosaic patt for leg. For both sizes work rnds 1–32 mosaic patt twice. Then work rnds 1–14 (1–30) once more.

Heel Flap

With A, cont in established patt and work 33 (39) sts for instep, (moving 1 st from heel side to instep). Knit 31 (37) sts. Cut B, leaving end long enough to weave in. There are 33 (39) instep sts, and 31 (37) heel sts.

Heel flap is worked back and forth beg on WS.

Using smaller needles and A, beg 2-color Eye of Partridge heel flap.

Row 1 (WS): With A, sl 1, P30 (36).

Row 2: With B, sl 1, K1, *K1, sl 1; rep from * to last 3 sts, K3.

Row 3: With B, sl 1, purl across.

Row 4: With A, sl 1, *K1, sl 1; rep from * to last 2 sts, K2.

Row 5: With A, sl 1, purl across.

Rep rows 2–5 until heel flap is 2⅜ (2½)" or desired length, ending with completed row 5.

With A, knit 1 row even.

Heel Turn

With A, turn heel as follows.

Row 1: Sl 1, P17 (21), P2tog, P1, turn.

Row 2: Sl 1, K6 (8), ssk, K1, turn.

Row 3: Sl 1, P7 (9), P2tog, P1 turn.

Row 4: Sl 1, K8 (10), ssk, K1, turn.

Rep rows 3 and 4, working 1 additional knit or purl st after the sl 1 until all side sts are worked. There are 19 (23) heel sts. Do not turn work.

Gusset

(If picking up more/fewer sts in heel, always inc or dec by 2 sts.)

Needle 1: 19 (23) sts are on needle. Using larger needles and A, pm to indicate start of gusset. PU 21 (23) sts along side of heel.

Needles 2 and 3: Work instep sts as established, and then knit the 33rd (39th) st on instep.

Needle 4: PU 21 (23) sts along rem side of heel.

Gusset Decrease

Rnd 1 with B

Needle 1: K19 (23) sole sts in mosaic patt for sole, sm, (sl 1, K1) 9 (10) times, K1, K2tog—39 (45) sts.

Needles 2 and 3: Work 33 (39) instep sts in established patt.

Needle 4: Ssk, K1 (K1, sl 1) 9 (10) times— 20 (22) sts.

Rnd 2 with B

Needle 1: K19 (23) sole sts in mosaic patt for sole, sm, knit to end.

Needles 2 and 3: Work instep sts in established patt.

Needle 4: Knit.

Rnd 3 with A

Needle 1: Knit 19 (23) sole sts in mosaic patt for sole, sm, (K1, sl 1). 8 (9) times, K2, K2tog—38 (44) sts.

Needles 2 and 3: Work instep sts in established patt.

Needle 4: Ssk, K1 (K1, sl 1) 8 (9) times, K1—19 (21) sts.

Rnd 4 with A

Needle 1: K19 (23) sole sts in mosaic patt for sole, sm, knit to end.

Needles 2 and 3: Work instep sts in established patt.

Needle 4: Knit.

Rep rnds 1–4 until 33 (37) total sole sts rem, plus instep sts, for a total of 66 (76) sts.

Foot

Cont working as established on 19 (23) sole sts, 7 gusset sts, 33 (39) instep sts, and 7 gusset sts, until foot measures about 2 (2¼)" less than desired length, ending on rnd 2 of mosaic patt for sole. Note that the gusset sts are worked in 2-color eye of partridge st as established.

COLOR FOR TOE

If your finished foot length is longer than 10½" or you made the leg longer than stated in the patt, you might want to wait to finish the toe on the first sock to be sure you have enough yarn You can always knit the toe in a contrasting color.

Toe Shaping

Using smaller needles and A, knit 1 rnd (remove marker at start of sole).

Toe set-up rnd: Knit sts on needle 1, dec 0, (2) sts across instep on needles 2 and 3 (now renumbered to 3 and 4). Cut A, leaving end long enough to weave in. Beg of rnd is now at side of foot ready to work sole. Divide sole sts evenly onto needles 1 and 2.

Using smaller needles and B, work toe shaping as follows.

Rnd 1 (dec rnd)

Needle 1: K1, ssk, knit to end.

Needle 2: Knit to last 3 sts, K2tog, K1.

Needle 3: K1, ssk, knit to end.

Needle 4: Knit to last 3 sts, K2tog, K1.

Rnds 2–4: Knit.

Rnd 5: As rnd 1. Cut yarn B, leaving end long enough to weave in.

With A,

Rnds 6 and 7: Knit.

Rnd 8: As rnd 1.

Rnds 9 and 10: Knit

Rnd 11: As rnd 1.

Rnd 12: Knit.

Rep rnds 11 and 12 twice more.

Rep rnd 1 until 18 (22) total sts rem. Graft toe sts tog using Kitchener st (see page 73) or desired grafting method. Weave in ends.

MOSAIC PATTERN— INTERLACING STRIPE FOR LEG AND INSTEP

The Small sock has an all-around pattern on the leg. The Large sock will have two mosaic panels separated by a smaller mosaic motif. Because you need a specific stitch count to make the pattern work, adjust the size by using smaller or larger needles.

On the right-hand side of the chart is a column of white and black squares separated by a blank column. Do not work the stitch in this column, but refer to this first column when working the charts. The basic rule is that on all rounds that begin with a white square, you knit white squares, and slip the black squares. On all rounds that begin with a black square, you knit the black squares and slip the white squares. All even-numbered rounds are worked as the odd-numbered rounds preceding them. All slipped stitches are worked by slipping as if to purl with yarn in back.

Rep rounds 1–32 for pattern.

Mosaic Pattern

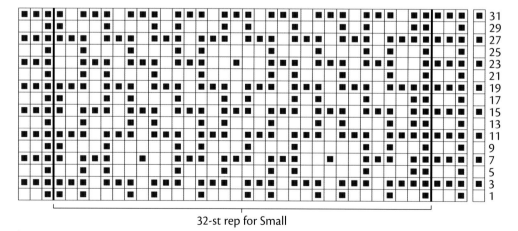

Key
- ■ Yarn A
- □ Yarn B

32-st rep for Small

38-st rep for Large

Only odd-numbered rnds are shown on chart.
All even-numbered rnds are worked as odd-numbered rnds.

ABBREVIATIONS AND GLOSSARY

approx	approximately
beg	begin(ning)(s)
BO	bind off
cn	cable needle
CO	cast on
cont	continue(ing)(s)
dec(s)	decrease(ing)(s)
dpn(s)	double-pointed needle(s)
g	grams
garter st	garter stitch: in the round—knit 1 round, purl 1 round
inc(s)	increase(ing)(s)
K	knit
K1f&b	knit into front and back of a stitch—1 stitch increased
K1 tbl	knit through back loop of stitch
K2tog	knit 2 stitches together—1 stitch decreased
kw	knitwise
LH	left hand
M1	make 1: Insert left-hand needle from front to back under horizontal strand between last stitch and next stitch, and knit it through back of loop.
M1P	make 1 purl: pick up horizontal strand as for M1, but purl into the back of the loop.
m	meters
mm	millimeters

oz	ounces
P	purl
P1f&b	purl into front and back of a stitch or yarn over—1 stitch increased
P2tog	purl 2 stitches together—1 stitch decreased
PfKb	purl into front of stitch and leave on needle, knit into back of stitch and slip both stitches off needle
patt(s)	pattern(s)
pm	place marker
psso	pass slipped stitch over
PU	pick up and knit
rem	remain(ing)(s)
rep(s)	repeat(s)
RH	right hand
rnd(s)	round(s)
RS	right side (outside of sock)
sk	skip
skp	slip 1 knitwise, knit 1, pass slipped stitch over—1 stitch decreased
sk2p	slip 1 knitwise, knit 2 stitches together, pass slipped stitch over the knit 2 together—2 stitches decreased
sl	slip
sl 1	slip 1 stitch as if to purl with yarn in back unless otherwise instructed
sm	slip marker

ssk	slip 2 stitches knitwise, 1 at a time, to right needle, then insert left needle from left to right into front loops and knit 2 stitches together—1 stitch decreased
ssp	slip 2 stitches, one at a time, as if to knit, return the 2 stitches back to left needle, purl 2 stitches together through the back loops—1 stitch decreased
sssp	slip, slip, slip, purl: slip 3 stitches, one at a time, as if to knit, return the 3 stitches back to the left needle, purl 3 stitches together through the back loops—2 stitches decreased
st(s)	stitch(es)
St st	stockinette stitch: in the round—knit every round; back and forth—knit 1 row, purl 1 row
tbl	through back loop(s)
tog	together
w&t	wrap and turn (see page 72)
WS	wrong side (inside of sock)
wyib	with yarn in back
wyif	with yarn in front
yds	yards
YO(s)	yarn over(s)

TECHNIQUES

The following techniques are used in this book.

Long-Tail Cast On

The long-tail cast on is elastic and sturdy. Use this technique when casting on for a sock that begins with ribbing.

Basic long-tail cast on. Make a slipknot with a tail about four times the length of the sock circumference. Or, starting at the end of the yarn, wrap the yarn around the needle the same number of times as the number of stitches you are casting on; make the slipknot there. The tail is the free end, and the long end is the yarn attached to the ball. Place the slipknot on the right-hand needle. Hold both lengths of yarn in the left hand, the tail over the thumb and the long end over the index finger. Both ends are tensioned by holding them in the palm with the other fingers (fig. 1). Insert the right-hand needle into the front of the loop on the thumb and over the yarn on the index finger (fig. 2). Bring this yarn through the loop on the thumb (fig. 3), forming a loop on the needle; tighten gently by placing the thumb under the yarn now coming from the needle and gently pulling back on it. This same motion sets up the loop on the thumb for the next stitch. Repeat for the required number of stitches.

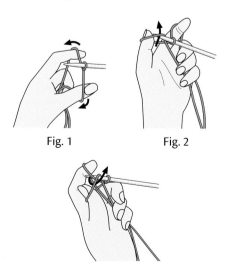

Fig. 1   Fig. 2

Fig. 3

Long-tail cast on for purl.

The basic long-tail cast-on method produces a knit stitch. It is possible to work a long-tail cast on as a purl. When you cast on in this manner for a K1, P1 ribbing or a K2, P2 ribbing, the cast-on edge becomes almost invisible, because the cast-on purled stitches recede as the purl stitches of the ribbing. To cast on in purl, begin as for regular long-tail cast on, but treat the loop on the thumb like a stitch on the left-hand needle, and the yarn around the index-finger like the yarn on a continental knitter's left finger when knitting. The motion of the needle and yarn is the same as making a purl stitch. Bring the needle behind the front strands of both loops (fig. 1). Catch the index-finger loop (fig. 2) and draw it through the thumb loop to complete the purl cast on (fig. 3). Repeat for the required number of stitches.

Working the knits and purls in the cast on gives you the option to work knit and purl sequences other than (K1, P1) or (K2, P2), such as for a 5-st ribbing patt like K1, P1, K1, P2.

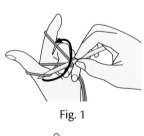

Fig. 1

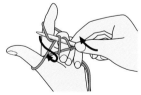

Fig. 2

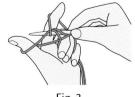

Fig. 3

Twisted German Cast On

This type of long-tail cast on provides more elasticity than the regular version. Begin as for basic long-tail cast on. Put the needle under both loops of the thumb yarn (fig. 1), pointing it toward the index finger. Bring the needle back into the loop just below the thumb and up toward you (fig. 2). Bend your thumb toward the index finger, twisting the loop with the needle through it so you can scoop the index-finger yarn back through the loop (fig. 3). Scoop the index-finger yarn back through the twisted loop (the loop that you just opened by bending your thumb). The index-finger yarn is through the thumb loop and is now on the needle. Drop the thumb loop off the thumb (fig. 4). Snug the yarns up against the needle. Repeat for the required number of stitches.

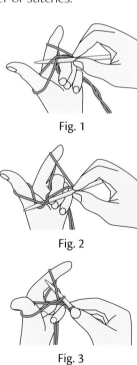

Fig. 1

Fig. 2

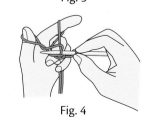

Fig. 3

Fig. 4

Knitted Cast On

Make a slipknot and place it on the left-hand needle. Insert the needle into the slipknot and knit a stitch (fig. 1); then place the new stitch on the left-hand needle as if to knit (fig. 2). *Knit into the first stitch on the left-hand needle and place the new stitch on the left-hand needle. Repeat from * for the required number of stitches.

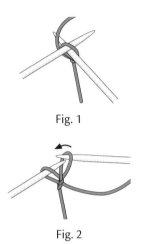

Fig. 1

Fig. 2

Becker Toe Cast On

This cast on was adapted from Judy Becker's "Magic Cast On for Toe-Up Socks," which was posted on www.knitty.com.

1. Make a slipknot and place the loop around one of the needles; this anchor stitch will count as one stitch. Hold the needles together, with the needle that the yarn is attached to toward the bottom. We'll call this needle 1 and the needle on the *top* needle 2.

2. In your other hand, hold the yarn so that the tail goes over your index finger and the working yarn (the yarn that leads to the ball) goes over the thumb. This is opposite from how the yarn is usually held for a long-tail cast on.

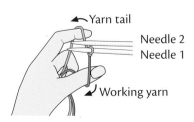

Yarn tail

Needle 2
Needle 1

Working yarn

3. Bring the tip of needle 2 (top needle) over the strand of yarn on your thumb, around and under the yarn and back up, making a loop around needle 2; pull the loop snug, but not too tight around the needle. This is the first stitch cast on needle 2, and original stitch cast on needle 1.

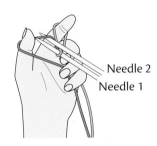

Needle 2
Needle 1

4. Bring needle 1 over the yarn tail on your index finger, around and under the yarn and back up, making a loop around needle 1. Pull the loop snug around the needle. You have cast on one stitch onto needle 1. There are now two stitches on needle 1 (the stitch you just cast on plus the anchor loop).

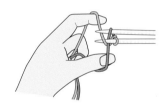

Remember: The top yarn (on the index finger) wraps around needle 1 (bottom needle), and the bottom yarn (the yarn around your thumb) always wraps around needle 2 (top needle).

Repeat steps 3 and 4 until you have the required number of stitches indicated in the pattern.

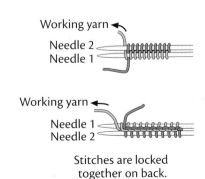

Working yarn

Needle 2
Needle 1

Working yarn

Needle 1
Needle 2

Stitches are locked together on back.

Continue as directed in the pattern. Knit across needle 1 (bottom needle), and then knit each stitch in the back of the loop on needle 2 (top needle).

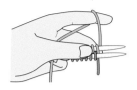

Turkish Cast On

Hold two double-pointed needles parallel and wrap the yarn in a figure eight around the needles until there are four (or number specified in pattern) loops on each needle (fig. 1). Hold the tail down with your left thumb, and use a third needle to knit the loops off the top needle without letting the loops on the bottom needle slide off (fig. 2). Turn, with another needle, knit the loops off the bottom needle through the back of the loop to keep them from being twisted. Knit the stitches on each needle one more time. Continue with instructions for your sock.

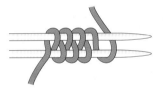

Fig. 1

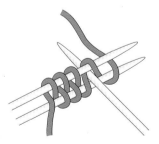

Fig. 2

Knitting with One Circular Needle

This method allows you to knit in the round using only one needle—a long circular needle with a flexible cable. Cast on the required number of stitches. Find the halfway point of the stitches and pull the cable out at that point to make a loop. Half the stitches are now on the front part of the cable and half are on the back. With the needle tips facing toward the right, pull the back needle out far enough to knit the stitches on the front cable. When the front stitches are all worked, turn the work so the needle tips are facing right once again. Work the second half of the stitches just as you did the first half.

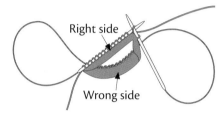

Wrap and Turn (w&t)

Wrap and turn is used in short rows. On the right side, when you come to the stitch to be wrapped, bring the yarn forward, slip the stitch purlwise to your working needle, bring yarn to back, turn work, and slip the stitch purlwise back to first needle (which is now the working needle).

On the wrong side, when you come to the stitch to be wrapped, bring the yarn to the back, slip the stitch purlwise to the working needle, bring the yarn forward, turn the work, and slip the stitch purlwise back to the first needle (which is now the working needle).

Avoiding Gap at the Top of Gusset

The hole or gap at the top of the gusset is a perennial problem for sock knitters. Some instructions do not provide any suggestion for how to alleviate this situation, and some suggest picking up one stitch, without any specifics on exactly where or how to do this.

We like to pick up two extra stitches at the top of the gusset. The way to identify these stitches is to look for the horizontal thread between the first instep stitch and the heel-flap stitch. Insert the needle into the left half of the heel-flap stitch and pick up one stitch; then pick up the right half of the first instep stitch from the row below the stitch on the needle. Both of these stitches are on the gusset needle.

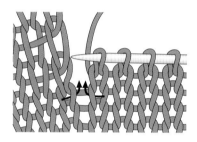

Picking up on knit sts

When picking up the gusset stitches on the other side of the sock, again locate the horizontal thread between the instep and heel flap; pick up the outside halves of each stitch and place them on the needle to be used for the heel gusset. If these stitches have been purled, just pick them up through the purl bump. These two extra stitches are worked together on the first gusset rnd.

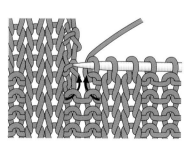

Picking up on purl sts

Bind Offs for Toe-Up Socks

These bind-off techniques are used at the top of the cuff when working a sock from the toe up. Just as you want a cast on for top-down socks that is loose and elastic, the bind off needs to be at least as elastic as the fabric and the same size. Some look similar to the standard bind off and some are decorative.

Standard Bind Off

Work two stitches; with the left-hand needle, pull the first stitch over the second stitch and off the needle. *Work another stitch and pull the previous one over it. Repeat from * to end.

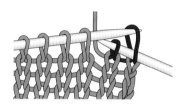

Suspended Bind Off

This bind off helps keep the stitches even on the bound-off edge. It also keeps the edge from becoming too tight or the stitches from stretching unevenly. Begin as for the standard bind off, but keep the lifted stitch on the left-hand needle, and then work the next stitch on the left-hand needle. Then slip off both the suspended stitch and new stitch together in one movement. This will leave two stitches on the right-hand needle. Draw the first stitch over the second and retain on the left-hand needle as before, and so on. Continue to end.

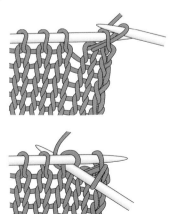

Decrease Bind Off

This produces another even bound-off edge. Knit the first stitch. *Slip the next stitch knitwise, insert the left needle into the front of the two stitches on the right needle and knit the two stitches together. One stitch remains on the right-hand needle. Repeat from * to end.

Frilled Bind Off

This bind off doubles the number of stitches during the bind-off round, making a very loose or frilled edge. To bind off, work the first stitch, M1, bind off the first stitch. *Work the next stitch on the left-hand needle, bind off, M1, bind off. Repeat from * to end.

Picot Bind Off

This bind off adds elasticity to the bound-off edge without the picots being very visible. To bind off, *cast on 1 stitch, using the "Knitted Cast On" (see page 71).

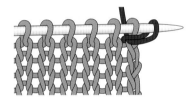

Cast on one stitch
using knitted cast on.

Then bind off 3 stitches, using the standard bind off, place the remaining stitch that is on the right-hand needle back on the left-hand needle. Repeat from * to end.

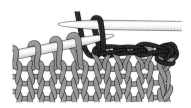

Bind off three stitches, then slip
stitch on right needle to left needle.

Sewn Bind-Off

This bind off creates a new stitch by weaving the yarn in and out of the knitting edge stitches. Cut the working yarn three or four times the circumference of the cuff and thread it onto a tapestry needle. To bind off, *insert the needle into the first two stitches from right to left (as if to purl); gently pull the yarn through the stitches.

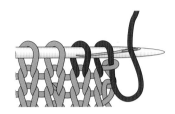

Insert the needle into the first stitch again, this time from left to right (as if to knit), and slip it off the needle. Gently pull the yarn through the stitch. Repeat from * to end.

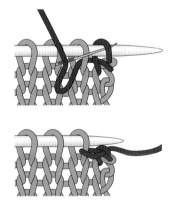

Grafting or Kitchener Stitch

Use this technique to sew the ends of the toes together. Work with the two pieces on the needles with wrong sides together, one needle behind the other. Thread a tapestry needle with the yarn attached to the back needle and work as follows:

Insert the tapestry needle into the first stitch of the front needle as if to purl, pull the yarn through but leave the stitch on the knitting needle. Go to the back needle, being careful to take the yarn under the knitting needle each time. Insert the tapestry needle into the first stitch as if to knit, pull the yarn through but leave the stitch on the knitting needle.

*Insert the tapestry needle into the first stitch of the front needle as if to knit, and then slip this stitch off the needle. Insert the yarn needle into the next stitch of the front needle as if to purl, pull the yarn through but leave the stitch on the knitting needle.

Go to the back needle and insert the yarn needle into the first stitch as if to purl. Take this stitch off and onto the tapestry needle. Put the tapestry needle through the next stitch of the back needle as if to knit. Pull the yarn through, but leave this stitch on the knitting needle. *

Rep from * to * until all stitches are joined. Do not draw the yarn too tightly. The stitches should have the same tension as the knitted stitches. Fasten the end securely.

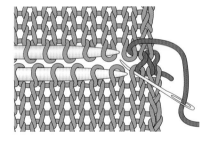

Here's a shorthand way of remembering how the grafting is done:

Front needle: Knit off, purl on.
Back needle: Purl off, knit on.

FOOT MEASUREMENTS

It is helpful to know the foot circumference, the length of the foot, the height of the leg you want to knit, and the height of the heel. If the socks are for you, it's easy to measure your bare foot. If you cannot measure the recipient's foot, we've included charts for women and men based on shoe size.

SIZE CHART FOR WOMEN								
	Foot Circumference in Inches			Sock Length in Inches				
Shoe Size	Narrow	Medium	Wide	Leg	Heel Flap	Heel to toe	Toe	Total Foot Length
5	6⅝	7½	8⅜	6⅛	2	7⅛	1⅝	8¾
5½	6¾	7⅝	8½	6¼	2	7¼	1⅝	8⅞
6	6⅞	7¾	8¾	6¼	2⅛	7¼	1¾	9
6½	7⅛	7⅞	8¾	6½	2⅛	7½	1¾	9¼
7	7¼	8⅛	9	6½	2¼	7⅝	1¾	9⅜
7½	7¼	8¼	9⅛	6¾	2¼	7¾	1¾	9½
8	7½	8⅜	9¼	6¾	2¼	8	1¾	9¾
8½	7⅝	8½	9⅜	6⅞	2¼	8	1¾	9¾
9	7¾	8¾	9½	7	2¼	8	2	10
9½	7⅞	8¾	9¾	7¼	2¼	9¼	2	10¼
10	8⅛	9	9¾	7¼	2¼	9¼	2	10¼
10½	8¼	9⅛	10	7⅜	2⅜	8½	2	10½
11	8⅜	9¼	10⅛	7⅝	2⅜	8¾	2	10¾
11½	8½	9⅜	10¼	7¾	2⅜	8¾	2	10¾
12	8¾	9½	10⅜	7⅞	2⅜	9	2	11

SIZE CHART FOR MEN								
	Foot Circumference in Inches			Sock Length in Inches				
Shoe Size	Narrow	Medium	Wide	Leg	Heel Flap	Heel to toe	Toe	Total Foot Length
6	7¼	8¼	9⅛	6½	2⅛	7⅝	1¾	9⅜
6½	7½	8⅜	9¼	6¾	2⅛	7¾	1⅞	9⅝
7	7⅝	8½	9⅜	6¾	2¼	7¾	2	9¾
7½	7¾	8¾	9½	6⅞	2¼	7¾	2	9¾
8	7⅞	8¾	9¾	7	2¼	8	2	10
8½	8⅛	9	9¾	7⅛	2¼	8¼	2	10¼
9	8⅛	9⅛	10	7¼	2¼	8¼	2	10¼
9½	8⅜	9¼	10⅛	7⅜	2⅜	8½	2⅛	10⅝
10	8½	9⅜	10¼	7½	2⅜	8⅝	2⅛	10¾
10½	8¾	9½	10⅜	7⅝	2⅜	8¾	2⅛	10⅞
11	8¾	9¾	10⅝	7¾	2½	8⅞	2⅛	11
11½	9	9¾	10¾	7¾	2½	8⅞	2¼	11⅛
12	9⅛	10	10⅞	7⅞	2⅝	8⅞	2⅜	11¼
12½	9¼	10⅛	11	8⅛	2⅝	9⅛	2⅜	11½
13	9½	10¼	11¼	8¼	2⅝	9¼	2⅜	11⅝
13½	9¾	10⅜	11¼	8¼	2¾	9⅜	2⅜	11¾
14	9¾	10⅝	11½	8⅜	2¾	9⅝	2⅜	12
14½	9¾	10¾	11⅝	8⅝	2¾	9¾	2⅜	12⅛
15	10	10⅞	11¾	8¾	2¾	9⅞	2⅜	12¼

USEFUL INFORMATION

Standard Yarn-Weight System						
Yarn-Weight Symbol and Category Names	**1** SUPER FINE	**2** FINE	**3** LIGHT	**4** MEDIUM	**5** BULKY	**6** SUPER BULKY
Types of Yarns in Category	Sock, Fingering, Baby	Sport, Baby	DK, Light Worsted	Worsted, Afghan, Aran	Chunky, Craft, Rug	Bulky, Roving
Knit Gauge Ranges in Stockinette Stitch to 4"	27 to 32 sts	23 to 26 sts	21 to 24 sts	16 to 20 sts	12 to 15 sts	6 to 11 sts
Recommended Needle in U.S. Size Range	1 to 3	3 to 5	5 to 7	7 to 9	9 to 11	11 and larger
Recommended Needle in Metric Size Range	2.25 to 3.25 mm	3.25 to 3.75 mm	3.75 to 4.5 mm	4.5 to 5.5 mm	5.5 to 8 mm	8 mm and larger

Skill Levels

■□□□ **Beginner:** Projects for first-time knitters using basic knit and purl stitches; minimal shaping.

■■□□ **Easy:** Projects using basic stitches; repetitive stitch patterns, and simple color changes; simple shaping and finishing.

■■■□ **Intermediate:** Projects using a variety of stitches, such as basic cables and lace, simple intarsia, and techniques for double-pointed needles and knitting in the round; midlevel shaping.

■■■■ **Experienced:** Projects using advanced techniques and stitches, such as short rows, Fair Isle, more intricate intarsia, cables, lace patterns, and numerous color changes.

Metric Conversions

Yards x .91 = meters
Meters x 1.09 = yards
Grams x .035 = ounces
Ounces x 28.35 = grams

YARN SOURCES

Cascade Yarns
www.cascadeyarns.com
Bollicine Dolly

Chewy Spaghetti
Khris Rogers
www.oneplanetyarnandfiber.com/
www.chewyspaghetti.etsy.com
Hand Painted Spaghetti II

Crazy4Dyeing
Ellie Putz
www.crazy4dyeing.com
Creamy Sock

Dale of Norway
www.dale.no.com
Baby Ull

Fearless Fibers
Deb Kessler
www.fearlessfibers.blogspot.com
www.etsy.com/shop.php?user_
  id=32548
Superwash Merino Wool Sock Yarn

Knit It Up (Sock Yarn Cinema)
Kate McMullin
www.knititupyarns.blogspot.com/
www.etsy.com/shop.php?user_
  id=5114588
Squishy Sock

Knit One Crochet Two
www.knitonecrochettoo.com
Soxx Appeal

Knit Picks
www.knitpicks.com
Stroll

**Lisa Souza Knitwear
  and Dyeworks**
www.lisaknit.com
Hand Dyed Sock! Yarn

Mama Llama Knits
Catherine Kerth
www.mamallamaknits.com
Mama Llama Original Sock 3ply

Misti International, Inc.
www.mistialpaca.com/
Misti Alpaca Lace

Simply Socks Yarn Company
www.simplysockyarn.com
Lang Jawoll Superwash

Tradewind Knitwear Designs
www.lucyneatby.com/yarn_store.html
Celestial Merino

Unicorn Books and Crafts, Inc.
www.unicornbooks.com
Lana Grossa Meilenweit

The Unique Sheep
www.theuniquesheep.com
Foot Prints
Sushi Sock
Verve

Wendy/Peter Pan
Thomas B. Ramsden & Co
www.tbramsden.co.uk/
Classic Courtelle 4 Ply
(Only available in UK or from UK
  sources)

Zen Yarn Garden
www.zenyarngarden.com
Cashmere Sock Yarn
Squooshy Yarn

Sock Clubs

ART WALK Sock YarnClub

Zen Yarn Garden handpaints yarns in colorways to match paintings of some of the world's greatest artists, recently including *Person at the Window* (Salvador Dali), *Fulfillment* (Gustav Klimt) and *Le Pont Japonais a Giverny* (Claude Monet). Each month, club members receive yarn, a sock pattern, an insert about each artist, and the painting. Yarns vary monthly, and membership is on a month-to-month basis.

Chewy Spaghetti's Blue Plate Special Monthly Sock Club

This club began in response to customer demand. The club has been discontinued. Watch Khris Rogers' knitting blog, www.chewyspaghetti. blogspot.com for announcements, wholesale information, and other news related to Chewy Spaghetti Hand-Dyed Yarns.

Crazy4Seasons Sock Club

Crazy4Seasons Sock Club ran for a year, beginning in the winter of 2007. There are twice as many members in Crazy as a Loon Sock Club for the current year. Each yarn package includes a sock pattern and either a set of stitch markers or a handmade sock-project bag.

Holiday Mystery Gifts KAL

Since 2007, this Yahoo! Group, with more than 1,500 members, has provided knitters and crocheters with unexpected patterns, shared expertise, and a place to post finished projects. Most designs are created by Terry Morris or Mindy Albright. Often the patterns are provided as a series of "clues" over time, with the final project a mystery to the participant. The online chat and support encourages participants to try a challenging project. The KAL is active September–December each year.

TheKnitter.com Sock of the Month Club

TheKnitter.com's sock club was one of the first, beginning April 2002. Several members have participated since the first kit. Each kit contains carefully selected yarn and a pattern written especially for the club. Members' monthy or bimonthly kits contain new and unique yarns, and patterns with a wide variety of different techniques. Recently, at the request of customers, a quarterly Luxury Sock Club has been added, featuring mostly handpainted yarns.

Knitting Central Sock Club

Sponsored by Knitting Central in Westport, Connecticut, this sock club provides members with unique socks designed by the staff members and teachers they know from the store. In addition to a pattern, each package includes a quality sock yarn carried in the store, a letter from the designer with a tip or technique, and a special little gift. A private Yahoo! Group allows members to ask questions and share information and pictures of their projects.

Scary Sock KAL

The Scary Sock KAL is a group of like-minded knitters on Ravelry who love old-fashioned horror films like the Hammer films. They knit socks related to the theme. Janine Le Cras has designed three socks for this KAL: Black Widow Spider, Revenge of the Mummies, and Gothic Temptress.

Seven Deadly Sins Sock Club

Fearless Fibers' Seven Deadly Sins Sock Club was offered by Deborah Kessler in the latter half of 2007 and was a small club limited to 50 members. Available slots sold out in just a few days. The club ran for four months, with the first three shipments each comprised of two skeins of Fearless Fibers Superwash Merino Wool Sock Yarn in colorways inspired by the Seven Deadly Sins. The fourth shipment included the final sin-inspired colorway (Greed) and the Acorn Stash Sock patt.

Seven Deadly S(p)ins Sock Club

A sock club based on the Seven Deadly Sins from Kelly Eells and Laura Bullins at Unique Sheep. Seven colorways of yarn and seven different sock designs from seven amazing designers sent every other month. Fun accessories were included in each to complement the yarn, pattern, and themes. Greed, Envy, Gluttony, Sloth, Pride, Wrath, and Lust! Hoarding is not on the list, so adding to your stash is acceptable. Gluttony was first in the series and is knit with yarn from the Gradiance collection.

Six Sox KAL

Six Sox KAL is a fairly large Yahoo! Group who get together to knit specially designed downloadable patterns that are only available to members. There is a new sock every two months, six a year, hence the name. This group also does an annual KAL of toddler socks for the charity Children in Common (CIC), which provides woollen socks to Russian orphanages.

Sockmaniac's Mystery Sock Club

Gail Dennis is Sockmaniac and founder of the club. She provides a pattern—a set of written pattern stitches to use to design a sock. No chart. No pictures. This is the mystery. Each member decides toe-up or cuff-down, type of heel and toe, how wide or narrow and where and how to use the pattern. Members come from around the world and share pointers—for example, a way to make a better heel flap came from a lady from the Netherlands—and lots of sharing and support.

SUMPTUOUS Sock Yarn Club

SUMPTUOUS Sock Yarn Club is a Zen Yarn Garden sock club focused on knitting with luxurious and exotic yarns such as cashmere, cashmere blends, and silk. Wrap your feet in pure luxury!

Woolgirl Sock Club

Woolgirl Sock Club is sponsored by Woolgirl, an online indie yarn shop created by Jennifer Jett. The club promotes indie dyers, new sock designers, and fun themes. The club has more than 300 members from over 20 countries and offers a bimonthly shipment, including sock yarn, a pattern featuring the yarn (sometimes 2 patterns or different yarn-weight options), a stitch marker, and unique knitting accessories from a variety of indie artists.

Designers

Judy Alexander
A lifelong love of fiber began when Judy learned to knit from her grandmother at the age of 10. This love of fiber has lead to an interest in weaving, spinning, beading, sewing, and quilting. After a long career as owners of a gift store, Judy and her husband created www.theknitter.com, an online yarn store specializing in sock and lace-weight yarns. Judy recently began designing patterns for socks, mittens, children's sweaters, and adult's sweaters. When not involved with her fiber-related activities, Judy enjoys spending time with her four children and five grandchildren.

Aliyya Behles
An advanced-practice registered nurse, Aliyya teaches at a school of nursing, but her real passions are knitting, spinning, and designing. She has knit since age nine and designed for herself, family, and friends for years. Recently, Blue Moon Fiber Arts and Woolgirl have used her patterns, and she has contributed to the Twisted Sisters' sweaters and socks books. If she had her way, she would be a fiber artist and indulge in all of wool's beauty, tactile sensations, smells, and inspirations. She recently relocated from the Pacific Northwest to Los Angeles, where she lives with her new husband.

Lisa Dykstra
Lisa is a creative fiber artist who currently resides in western Michigan with her husband and three children. She credits her love of crafting to her talented mother and grandmothers, who encouraged her from a very young age. Lisa enjoys designing socks and lace and loves sharing her passion for knitting and spinning with others. She works and designs part time to support her fiber habit. Her designs can be found at Woolgirl, Crystal Palace Yarns, Ravelry, and her blog, www.ayenforyarn.blogspot.com.

Kelly Eells
A fiber enthusiast for over 20 years, Kelly Eells learned to crochet from her grandmother and taught herself to knit. Fifteen years ago she met Menke Saarniit, her best friend and mentor, who taught her to spin, weave, and hand dye yarns and fibers. After years of dyeing, Kelly found a dye partner in Laura Bullins.

Kelly's Liisu Yarns merged with Laura's The Unique Sheep in late 2007. Kelly lives with her husband and two dogs in North Carolina, where she enjoys going to the gym, working on stained glass and tile mosaics, and listening to podcasts in her basement studio.

Adrienne Fong
Adrienne did not initially understand all the fuss about hand-knit socks. After knitting her first pair of socks about five years ago, she "got" it and has since been working on her sock-yarn collection. She is hopelessly attempting to finish the mates to her collection of "one" socks. She has designed socks for TheKnitter, Blue Moon Fiber Arts, Crystal Palace Yarns, PT Yarns, SWTC, and Robyn's Nest.ca. Adrienne blogs at http://bellybuttonknits.blogspot.com and can be found on Ravelry as "bellybuttonknits."

Bindu Gupta
Bindu Gupta teaches computer science at Roosevelt University in Chicago. She has been knitting since age nine and likes the challenge of sock knitting. Her design developed from an August 2008 pattern at Sockmaniac's Mystery Sock Club on Yahoo!. The club's stitch patterns are fabulous, and as they are knit up, the pattern unfolds. Bindu is very involved in charity knitting with the group Merry Makers, which knits for homeless shelters and a South Dakota reservation, and with Children in Common, which knits for orphanages in Russia and Kazakhstan.

Anne Hanson
Knitspot owner and designer Anne Hanson, a lifelong knitter, enjoys an ongoing conversation with users, incorporating their feedback into Knitspot products. Anne's background as a pattern maker/draper, technical designer, and costumer in New York City's garment district informs her work, providing a rich source of experience in garment construction and fit, as well as a wide range of fibers and fabrics. Anne also teaches and writes about knitting, spinning, and designing on her blog at http://www.knitspot.com. She lives in Ohio with David, who loves wool, too.

Alyson Johnson
Alyson Johnson is a knitter, spinner, dyer, instructor, and designer in Florida, where wool socks are an absolute

necessity—for three entire days a year. She's had a growing obsession with fiber arts since 2004. While she can't quite remember how she started designing, it likely began with a mistake that was dubbed a "design element." Inspiration for her designs comes from color, architecture, and nature (and random experimentation and blatant mistakes). She lives with her very patient husband, who agreed to learn to knit just so she'd shut up about it already.

Emily Johnson
Emily Johnson is a published knitwear designer living in Portland, Oregon. Her designs are often inspired by vintage styles and include unique or evocative touches. She and her partner, David Galli, are working on a longterm exploration of family history through knitting design; her writing, knitting, and design work can be found at the Family Trunk Project (http://www.familytrunkproject.com). She has always loved the storytelling potential of clothes and considers friends, pets, favorite places, and fictional characters to be part of her extended family as well.

Janine Le Cras
Janine Le Cras lives on the tiny island of Guernsey in the middle of the English Channel. Famous for its cows and its knitting, Guernsey's residents knit socks for Queen Elizabeth I! Janine learned to knit at her grandmother's knee at age seven and has been designing for five years. Her patterns have been published by Magknits, Knotions, The Inside Loop, Six Sox KAL, Scary Socks KAL and SockMadness, and they will be in two books to be published in late 2009. A wife and the mother of grown-up children, Janine's day job in IT fortunately leaves time for her to knit, spin, and windsurf.

Ann McClure
Ann McClure has been crocheting since she was a child and knitting since 2001. She is a professional writer and editor who lives in Connecticut with her husband, Brian, and their two golden retrievers. She has worked at Knitting Central in Westport, Connecticut, since 2005 in order to have constant access to luxury yarn. Her work has also appeared in *Luxury Yarn One-Skein Wonders* (Storey Publishing, 2008). Ann blogs about her crafts and her dogs at www.travelingann.blogspot.com.

Emily B. Miller

Emily B. Miller lives in Chicago, where knitted socks have become an important part of her winter survival strategy. She loves learning and sees the fiber arts as a wonderful way to experiment with new concepts and techniques—since the outcome is usually something useful and warm. Emily is surrounded by family, bright colors, baking projects, and a cat who appreciates her knitting habit, since it keeps her lap stationary for extended periods of time! Emily's adventures in dyeing, sewing, and knitwear design can be found at www.SkylineChilly.com.

Terry Morris

Terry Liann Morris, aka SailingKnitter, lives full time aboard her 50-foot sailboat. Whether at anchor or sailing, Terry knits, designs knitting patterns, and knits some more. Terry, a CYCA Certified Knitting Instructor, has taught over 250 knitters how to knit or to how advance their skills. The history of knitting holds a special interest for Terry: Gansey, Fair Isle, or Aran styles show up in most of her designs. In addition to her self-published pattern line, SailingKnitter Liann Originals, Terry manages the Gansey List and Holiday Mystery Gifts Yahoo! groups.

Debbie O'Neill

Debbie is a software engineer, but spends her free time teaching knitting and writing knitting patterns. She loves to share knitting knowledge and will happily talk knitting for hours. Debbie designs for TheKnitter, The Loopy Ewe, and Cherry Tree Hill Yarns. Her designs appear in magazines, knitting books, and yarn-company publications. Debbie self-publishes her patterns under the name Nutty Creations. Her first book will be available in 2009. When she isn't knitting or working, Debbie spends time with her family, cooks, reads, and dabbles in other fiber pursuits.

Ellie Putz

Crazy4Dyeing is a one-woman show and the brainchild of Ellie Putz. A quilter for many years, she has come only lately to knitting and dyeing. Her experience with color served her well while designing and creating quilts, and now she puts those fine-tuned skills to good use while dyeing her unique colorways. A scientist by education, she forgoes formulas and note taking while dyeing and lets serendipity rule the day. It all seems just a little crazy!

Carol Schoenfelder

Carol Schoenfelder learned to crochet at about age 10, but didn't discover knitting until much later; her college roomate's mom was a professional knitter. Self-taught, Carol picked up what she could from store-bought and ball-band patterns and her first knitting book, *The Sweater Workshop* (Down East Books, 2002). After discovering the myriad of online resources, her knitting really took off. In 2006, she knit her first sock—and has been hooked ever since. After many moves, Carol now lives in Illinois with her husband and two cats.

Dyers

Kelly Eells (See Designer Bio)

Catherine Kerth

A passionate knitter, Catherine Kerth has been dying yarn, designing patterns and accessories, as well as teaching classes in Katy, Texas, for over four years. Her worldwide travels and challenging life experiences have inspired unique colorways and accessories that have become favorites amoung savvy knitters today. Features in *Knit It! Magazine* and in several sock clubs have helped Catherine develop her company, Mama Llama, into a thriving business that continues to expand. Catherine can be found online at www.mamallamaknits.com.

Deb Kessler

Deb Kessler is the indie dyer known as Fearless Fibers. She has knit since childhood and began her obsession with dyeing in 2003. Deb started Fearless Fibers after escaping from the corporate world in January 2006. With a focus on subtle and harmonious variations of color, Deb found her niche in sock and lace yarns that lend themselves to complex stitch work. She has happily spent her days surrounded by yarn and immersed in the world of knitting ever since. Deb resides in Oregon with her husband, Bruce, and their dog, Indie (named, of course, in honor of all indie dyers!).

Kate McMullin

Kate McMullin and her family-run company Knit It Up are based in rural New Mexico. They like keeping it small, so they can give special attention to every skein and create beautiful colorways that can't be found anywhere else. Sock Yarn Cinema grew out of Kate's love of movies, where she frequently finds inspiration for colorways. Each month club members are treated to a movie-inspired colorway, along with goodies and knitting tools that match the theme.

Ellie Putz (See Designer Bio)

Khris Rogers

Four years ago, Khris's son insisted she teach him to knit. She figured if a six-year-old could do it, she should be able to figure it out. She picked up yarn and needles and checked out a book from the library. By the time she "got" it, her son had lost interest, but she was hooked! A year later she started experimenting with dyeing yarn and became passionate about it. Her studies in fashion and costuming helped her with color theory and fiber knowledge, but mostly it was just plain fun. She hopes to open her own website soon. Until then you can find her at chewyspaghetti.etsy.com.

Lisa Souza

Artisan dyer and colorist, Lisa Souza, has created art-to-wear garments with hand-spun and hand-dyed yarn for over 25 years, selling her knitwear and yarns to collectors at juried craft shows in the West. Her indelibly personal color sense has garnered a loyal following that has translated to her yarn and fiber business, reaching the new wave of spinners and knitters around the world from her studio in Placerville, California. She can be found online at www.lisaknit.com.

Roxanne Yuen

Zen Yarn Garden is the labor of love for Roxanne Yeun in Ontario, Canada, where she lives with her darling husband, who is patient with the dye studio taking over his house. Roxanne is a knitter, spinner, and crocheter. She first dabbled in dyeing yarn in late 2005. It became her mission to provide passionate, inspirational, and creative colors to inspire every one of her customers. Roxanne's love of color keeps her motivated—she finds inspiration all around her, from the trees outside her window to the food on her plate. Roxanne's daily job is a truly wonderful and blessed one.

ABOUT THE AUTHORS

Charlene Schurch

Beth Parrott

Charlene Schurch is the author of a growing number of knitting books and numerous magazine articles about knitting. Her articles have appeared in *Vogue Knitting, Interweave Knits, Piecework,* and *Spin Off.* She divides her time between Connecticut and Florida.

Although Beth Parrott has been knitting for more than 60 years, until recently she designed socks and other garments only for family and for charity projects. She loves to teach and is an avid collector of tricks-of-the-trade and tidbits of information that make knitting easier. She works, plays, knits, and teaches in Charleston, South Carolina.

Other book by these authors:
Schurch, Charlene.
More Sensational Knitted Socks.
Woodinville, Washington: Martingale & Company, 2007.

Schurch, Charlene.
Sensational Knitted Socks. Woodinville, Washington:
Martingale & Company, 2005.

Schurch, Charlene and Beth Parrott. *The Little Box of Socks.*
Woodinville, Washington: Martingale & Company, 2008.